D1569785

CONFLICT AND POLITICS OF IDENTITY IN SUDAN

CONFLICT AND POLITICS OF IDENTITY IN SUDAN

AMIR H. IDRIS

CONFLICT AND POLITICS OF IDENTITY IN SUDAN

First published in 2005 by
PALGRAVE MACMILLAN™
175 Fifth Avenue, New York, N.Y. 10010 and
Houndmills, Basingstoke, Hampshire, England RG21 6XS
Companies and representatives throughout the world.

PALGRAVE MACMILLAN is the global academic imprint of the Palgrave Macmillan division of St. Martin's Press, LLC and of Palgrave Macmillan Ltd. Macmillan® is a registered trademark in the United States, United Kingdom and other countries. Palgrave is a registered trademark in the European Union and other countries.

ISBN 1–4039–6939–6

Library of Congress Cataloging-in-Publication Data

Idris, Amir H., 1962–
    Conflict and politics of identity in Sudan / by Amir Idris.
        p. cm.
    Includes bibliographical references and index.
    ISBN 1–4039–6939–6
        1. Sudan—Politics and government—1985– 2. Political culture—Sudan. 3. Political violence—Sudan. 4. Citizenship—Sudan. 5. Nationalism—Sudan. 6. National characteristics, Sudanese. 7. Sudan—Colonial influence. 8. Slavery—Sudan. I.Title.

JQ3981.A91I37 2005
962.4043—dc22   2005048683

A catalogue record for this book is available from the British Library.

Design by Newgen Imaging Systems (P) Ltd., Chennai, India.

First edition: August 2005

10 9 8 7 6 5 4 3 2 1

Printed in the United States of America.

Transferred to digital printing in 2007.

Contents

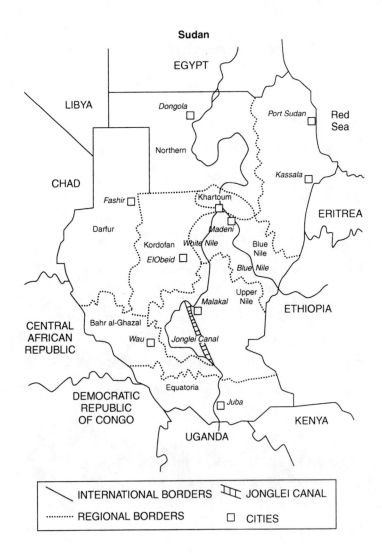

Abbreviations and Acronyms

GOS   Government of the Sudan
IGAD   Inter-Governmental Authority on Development
JEM   Justice and Equality Movement
NDA   National Democratic Alliance
NIF   National Islamic Front
OAU/AU   Organization of African Unity/African Union
SANU   Sudan African National Union
SLA   Sudan Liberation Army
SLM   Sudan Liberation Movement
SPLA   Sudan People's Liberation Army
SPLM   Sudan People's Liberation Movement

Preface

Since the 1980s, I have been studying and researching the causes of the civil war and its consequences in the Sudan. Two factors pushed me to embark on this academic journey at that time. First, the rising number of civilians who were killed as a result of the war or other war-related causes made me aware of the intensity and viciousness of the war. Second, the civil war also had a personal impact. In mid-1980s, I was able to meet my aunt for the first time in my life. It was also a memorable moment for my father who was reunited with his sister after more than two decades. But, this historical reunion became possible not as a result of a personal choice but rather as a consequence of the military regime policy of aggression and discrimination toward people of Southern Sudan. Like hundreds of thousands of Southern Sudanese civilians forced to flee the South, my aunt left Bahr al Ghazal to Wed Medani, a city in the Central Sudan, where her brother had lived for decades. Her long journey to the North not only made me realize the extent of the human suffering in the South, but also the determination of those who were subjected to oppression and racism to make the North their refuge. Indeed, the struggle in this context did not only mean the securing of basic needs but also the coexistence with other identities and histories.

Growing up in a family with multiple identities and histories indeed gave me the opportunity to observe how different cultures and traditions coexisted and reconciled in a shared space. This shared space has been made and remade by the involvement of all members of the family in spite of their cultural, traditional, and religious differences. Living in exile since 1990 has also introduced me to an intellectual space that is free from the constraints of culture, tradition, and boundary. This new intellectual space indeed enables me to reflect on and engage in rich and stimulating conversations centered on the politics of identity. In addition to my research and reading, my conversations with my students and colleagues, on race, racism, and the future of American democracy have drawn me into the field of comparative examination of these issues in different historical and political contexts. In the United States, it has become widely acceptable in academia today to argue that the problem of racism and inequality facing African Americans cannot be separated from the question of power, the state, and the allocation of resources. Consequently, there is increasingly less debate in the United States on race in the traditional sense.

In Africa, the spread of political violence has always been seen as a product of deep hatred embedded in the structures of war-torn societies. Race and ethnicity have been identified as major sources of the conflict. On the one hand, many people in the Sudan, especially from the Southern Sudan, have lost hope of finding a solution within the boundaries of the existing state. The solution for them is the construction of new states that reflect the "true" identity of these marginalized groups. On the other hand, those who belong to the dominant group, mostly from the North, believe that colonialism was the "inventor" of the crisis, and national unity can be cultivated if "southerners" free themselves from the colonial invention. The supporters of the latter position however have rejected any attempt at restructuring the inherited colonial state. Both discourses—separatist and integrationist—have dominated the political discussion on the nature and the future of the state in the Sudan. In the Sudan, race and ethnicity has been taken for granted, and no effort is made to locate them in their proper historical and political context. In turn, very little discussion exists on how struggle over histories and identities offer competing visions of peace and democracy in the region.

This book continues my previous conversations on the relationship among slavery, colonialism, and the construction of "Africanism" and "Arabism" as competing political identities in the Sudan.[1] This book, however, goes further to examine the relationship among histories, identities, and conflicts. The goal is to bring history and politics back into the discussion on civil war and the future of postcolonial citizenship in the Sudan. The purpose of the conversation is to identify some insights that could be drawn from the experiences of people of Southern and Western Sudan. I am aware of the different historical and political trajectories that shaped the realities of both regions. But, I am also convinced that the historical legacies of slavery and colonialism are central to the crisis of postcolonial citizenship in the Sudan. I hope this conversation will enable people of the Sudan to engage in long and constructive conversations that go beyond the colonial trap of ethnicity and race and to argue for a viable political project that embraces inclusive citizenship.

Acknowledgments

This study would not have been possible without the financial support for my fieldwork provided by the Department of History at Queen's University in Canada, and the Ford Foundation Regional Office in Cairo. I would also like to thank the Institute of African Studies at Columbia University in New York City for offering me a postdoctoral fellowship during the academic year 2000–2001. The postdoctoral fellowship enabled me to develop the theoretical framework for this work, which forms the basis of the book, and for providing me with a stimulating intellectual environment.

I wish to express my gratitude to Professor Robert Shenton for his ongoing enthusiasm and constructive criticism. I would also like to thank Dr. Taisier M. Ali, who has encouraged and supported my academic journey since the 1980s.

I am forever indebted to the Sudanese communities in Cairo, and particularly the peoples of Southern Sudan. They have shared with me their exile experiences and allowed me to participate in their daily lives. It is indeed impossible to forget their hospitality and kindness, offered under such harsh and unforgiving conditions.

At the Institute of African Studies of Columbia University, many colleagues assisted me in numerous ways during my post-doctoral fellowship. I would like to thank Joe Caurso, Marcia Wright, Paul Martin, Linda Beck, Greg Mann, and Kiki Edozie for their ongoing support, constructive conversations, and valuable suggestions. Special thanks to Professor Mahmood Mamdani, Director of the Institute of African Studies at Columbia University for sharing his ideas and comments during our stimulating biweekly seminar at the Institute. I derived great benefit from his suggestions and engaging criticism.

I am also grateful to my colleagues at Fordham University, in the Department of African and African American Studies. Special thanks to Irma Watkins-Owens, Mark Chapman, Mark Naison, and Claude Mangum for their support and encouragement.

This book is dedicated to my grandmother who refused to equate the state of being a refugee with being hopeless. She did not allow herself to be trapped in the official identity of "Western African immigrant" in central Sudan. Instead, she constructed a new life by transcending both the old and the new identity. Her lived experience surely taught me how to imagine the possibility of a new future built on accepting and recognizing the value of transcending our differences in a way that enriches our collective humanity.

INTRODUCTION

For over four decades, armed conflicts have been raging in the Sudan, with tragic consequences for social, economic, and political development. In contemporary times, the Sudan constitutes a major theater of political conflicts and civil wars. Political conflicts and civil wars are threatening to dismantle the postcolonial state in the Sudan. The consequences of these conflicts have been harmful to the country's growth, stability, and security.

The postcolonial state in the Sudan has endured long periods of violent conflicts, which have resulted in great human suffering and the largest number of refugees and displaced peoples in Africa. The Sudan, certainly, not only offers a good context for examining issues of competing visions of histories and identities but also illustrates clearly how the entrenchment of these issues have been accompanied by violent conflicts and claims to either restructuring the state or seeking separate states and nations. The armed struggles of peoples of the Southern Sudan and the recent violent conflict in the western region of Darfur are good examples. The civil war in the Sudan is often presented in essentially ethnic and religious terms: "Arab" Muslim North against "African" Christian South. The crisis in Darfur however demonstrated the failure of the North–South paradigm in explaining the historical and political causes of the conflict. In the context of "North–South" conflict in the Sudan, the people of Darfur are commonly considered Muslims and "northerners." Yet, like the people of the Southern Sudan, they have been oppressed, deprived, and are the least developed economically due to the century-old colonial subjugation and relentless exploitation. The recent violent attacks against some "non-Arab" Muslim groups such as the Fur, the Zaghawa, and the Massaleit in the western region of Darfur prove that conversion to Islam couldn't fully compensate for the absence of "an Arab origin" in the Sudan.[1]

The last decade of the twentieth century has witnessed growing interests on addressing the root causes of civil wars and the crisis of the African state.[2] Much of the debate has focused on examining the role of the colonial and the postcolonial states on triggering the tension and conflict between diverse ethnic groups in Africa. Sadly, Africa has often been perceived as "out of history." Its political violence seems to have no history and no politics, and hence is unthinkable. While some scholars have suggested that the root causes of the problem lie in the ethnic and "tribal" structures of the African societies,[3] others have emphasized the role of the colonial state on inventing and legalizing ethnic and racialized identities.[4] Much emphasis has been laid either on the colonial or the postcolonial period, but very little on the precolonial context. This tendency has led many scholars to suggest liberal democracy as a solution to the problem of civil wars and ethnic conflicts in Africa. For the last ten years, many African countries adopted democracy as a political mechanism to cope with growing political pressures, from within and without. The results were not impressive.[5] In some countries, such as Nigeria, Rwanda, the Sudan, and Ethiopia, violence has become widespread.

Much of the recent literature on Africa's political violence focuses on the prospects for democratic transition and the role of civil society in bringing about political stability and economic development in post-conflict societies.[6] However, few African countries have achieved a genuine democratic transition beyond a mere adoption of multiparty politics. The reason for this failure is that few African governing elites are ready to confront the past.

The focus should not simply be on what type of political system exists (democratic or nondemocratic) but rather on the foundation upon which it is laid. In other words, too much scholarship focuses on the institutions necessary for political democracy, but not enough explores the nature of the postcolonial state and the crisis of citizenship in postcolonial Africa.[7]

In northeast Africa, for instance, much of the contemporary debate on political violence and state reform remains focused on the transformation of political systems, on regime change, and electoral competition as preconditions for Western-style democracy.[8] These suggestions and perspectives are usually based on inadequate knowledge of histories, identities, and the dynamics of state formations in the region. Very little exists on how struggle over histories and identities offer competing visions of peace and stability. In the Sudan, the legacy of the past has certainly had a tremendous impact on the persisting current violent conflict between the nation-state and the subordinated groups in the country.[9]

This book explores the relationship among histories, politics of identities, and conflicts in the Sudan. The political violence in the Sudan is often perceived in essentially ethnic and religious terms: Arab Muslim Northern Sudanese against African Christian Southern Sudanese. In recent years, the question of "indignity" and "settlers" becomes central to the debate on the future of democratic citizenship in the postcolonial state in Africa.[10] In the Sudan, the term African is associated with "indigenous"/"native" peoples, while the term Arab often refers to "alien" or settlers. This dichotomy indeed has brought the question of citizenship and democratic rights to the forefront of contemporary debate on the future of the postcolonial state in the Sudan.

This book challenges the prevailing explanation that violent political conflict in the Sudan is a result of deep hatreds and ethnic loyalties. More specifically, it argues that this explanation is inadequate for understanding the nature of political conflict in contemporary Sudan. Alternatively, the disintegration of a state-building project and the spread of political violence in the Sudan can be understood only by locating the precolonial and the colonial legacies in the postcolonial context. The book specifically attempts to understand how an ideology of hierarchy, which assigned a subordinate status for the people of the Southern Sudan, was historically constructed and politically institutionalized.

The goal is to acknowledge the centrality of the historical legacy of slavery and colonialism in the crisis of postcolonial citizenship in the Sudan. In the Sudan, the legacies of slavery, the slave trade, and colonialism are particularly significant in understanding the interplay between the processes of state formation and nation-building, and the crisis of democratic citizenship and violence. Racialized and despotic states in the Sudan have had a crucial historical role in spreading violence in the Southern Sudan and more recently in the western region of Darfur. Despite the long history of slavery and slave trading by Arabs in the region of Northeast Africa, this legacy has been given less attention by scholars than warranted. Muslim scholars especially have written relatively little about this human tragedy. However, the painful history of slavery and violence in the region, and the Sudan in particular, has shown the difficulty of fostering democratic citizenship and political stability in the postcolonial state.

In the late 1970s and throughout the 1980s and the 1990s, scholars have tackled the challenges and developed an impressive literature on slavery in African societies.[11] However, little discussion has been focused on the relationship between the process of state formation and practice of slavery and the slave trade in the African continent. Contemporary debates on state, political identities, and conflicts have also ignored the legacy of slavery and the slave trade on complicating the process of nation-building in Africa. In the Sudan, contemporary conflicts over histories and identities cannot be understood without acknowledging the legacies of slavery and colonialism in shaping the relationship between the postcolonial state and marginalized ethnic groups. However, neither those who are included nor those who are excluded from the realm of democratic citizenship in the post-colonial state are ready to acknowledge the legacy of slavery in the contemporary discussion on political conflict and the disintegration of the postcolonial state in the Sudan.

The "Sudanese" state possesses certain historical characteristics. The dominant ruling groups claim the divine right of ruling their subjects on the basis of "historical unity" existing before recorded history. The ruling groups have used this myth of historical unity to legitimate the invented vision of nation-state, which was mostly supported by military power. In the Sudan, however, revolt against the state emerged first as political opposition to centralized/racialized despotism and demand for more inclusion in state institutions. Ruling groups, who often undermined the capacity of marginalized peoples to seek justice for past grievances, rejected such demands for inclusion. Many opportunities were missed to negotiate peaceful solutions, which could have prevented the escalation of political violence.[12] One of the factors that has contributed to this crisis was the lack of political commitment to extend the privilege of citizenship to marginalized peoples, something that would have created new norms and principles of governance. These historical characteristics became a source of political conflict that undermines the legitimacy of postcolonial regimes in the Sudan.

The Structure of the Book

The book is divided into six chapters. Chapter 1 attempts to reconceptualize the relationship between history, identity, and conflict. It examines the contemporary debate on conflict, peace, and political stability within the colonially inherited nation-states in Africa and the Sudan in particular. The chapter also explores the implications of existing competing visions of histories and identities on the processes of democratization and state-building.

Chapter 2 deals with the historical processes of state formation in the context of contested histories and identities and examines how different ethnic groups were incorporated into the project of the nation-state. The objective here is to rethink the emergence of a formative period of the Sudanese state, shifting the emphasis away from constructed homogeneous ethnic and racial categories, to understanding the constituents that went into its making. How is such a state and ethnic or racial groups constituted? How is the state integrated, economically, politically, and socially? This chapter in particular attempts to bring back history and politics into the understanding of the Sudan's tragedy. This Sudanese problem has been often perceived as a conflict between an Arab Muslim North and an African Christian or "animist" South.[13] Instead, I would argue that neither culture nor race is at the heart of the current conflict, rather it is the racialized state that transformed these cultural identities into political ones through the practice of slavery in the precolonial period, indirect rule during the colonial period, and state sponsored Islamization and Arabization in the postcolonial period. More specifically, the chapter explores the evolution of the political program of "Arabization" and "Islamization" as contested national projects in the Sudan. It discusses the integration of the precolonial process of enslavement and the nature of political identities generated during the colonial period.

Chapter 3 focuses on the emergence of the nationalist movements that are opposed to the exclusionary nation-state in the Sudan. The goal is to examine critically nationalist discourses of the Southern Sudanese. However, I argue that the nationalist movements in the Sudan have failed to transcend the colonially constructed racial and ethnic identities in their struggle for power and rights. This failure has contributed to the heightening of identity politics and conflict instead of institutionalizing democratic citizenship. Like the notion of nation, nationalism in Africa has always been contested both during the colonial and the postcolonial periods. Nationalism in the Sudan, for instance, was socially constructed, with distinct regional, ethnic, class, and gender orientations. It was true in case of the Sudan, not all Sudanese were engaged in the nationalist movement of the 1930s. The region of the Southern Sudan has been excluded from the realm of citizenship and rights and subjected to violence within the context of the Sudanese state.

Chapter 4 examines the experience of the Southern Sudanese refugees in Egypt and its implications for the transformation of identities and political reform in the Sudan.[14] My goal in this chapter is to problematize the different nationalist visions of identity that are advanced by southern nationalists in their liberation struggle against the postcolonial state to legitimize their claims for greater autonomy or independence. The study is based on an ethnographic case study completed in 1997 among the Southern Sudanese in Cairo, Egypt. The methods of participant observation, interviews, and the recording of the Southern Sudanese life histories in exile were used. The research suggests that the meaning of place of "origin" is neither constant nor essential, and that the shifting nature and meaning of place has serious implications for the formation of political and cultural identities. This case study not only presents us with another vision of identity but it also gives us an insight into understanding the postcolonial context of political identity as lived, felt, and observed by those who are affected by the violence. In this chapter, I argue that the crossing of borders, being away from home, has made a significant contribution to the emergence of new cultural and political identities among the refugees. As people experience these processes of displacement, their notions of self and society shift, and, in the process, they construct and reconstruct their own identities.

Chapter 5 examines the crisis in Darfur and its implications for a durable peace in the Sudan. Peace negotiations between the Government of the Sudan (GOS) and the Sudan People's Liberation Army/Movement (SPLA/M) are being framed as if they are about outstanding North–South conflicts over security, power and wealth sharing, and the future of the three contested regions. However, the north–south conflict is only one of the many regional conflicts that have devastated the Sudan.

Chapter 6 attempts to propose an alternative perspective of the politics of identity, conflict, and peace in the Sudan by examining critically the discourse on political participation and the discourse on power and citizenship in the context of contested histories and identities. The goal here is to go beyond the ancient traps of ethnicity and race and to argue for an inclusive alternative in democratic citizenship.

CHAPTER 1
RECONCEPTUALIZING HISTORY, IDENTITY, AND CONFLICT

Although many studies have sought to identify the underlying causes of the conflict in Africa, scholars have devoted less attention to analyzing the notion of citizenship in contested social and political settings.[1] Very few have grappled with the following theoretical and historical questions. How do competing visions of histories and identities shape the processes of conflict and the meaning of peace? Are current approaches to peace and democracy well suited to the task of consolidating peace in war-torn states? Does political competition according to rules of democratic pluralism in racialized states secure the democratic citizenship of the marginalized groups who were subjected to slavery and colonialism in the past? By addressing these questions, this chapter attempts to reconceptualize the relationship between history, identity, and peace in contested social and political settings.

The "liberal internationalism" discourse seems to guide the works of many scholars analyzing the relationship between conflict, democracy, and peace in Africa. The main premise of this discourse is that the building of peace and democracy in war-torn societies requires both the existence of a market economy and a liberal democratic government.[2] Peace, then, is in effect an experiment in social engineering that involves transplanting Western models of social, political, and economic organizations into war-torn societies in order to control civil conflict: in other words, pacification through political and economic liberalization.

This assumption is inadequate, particularly in the contexts of the Sudan. The process of political and economic liberalization is not only inherently disruptive but also shaped by the historical and cultural contexts of the given society. This approach also tends to ignore the fact that these conflicts have histories and politics. Instead, we should perceive the current conflicts within its proper historical and political contexts. The violent political conflicts in the Sudan are manifestations of legacies of the past, namely slavery and colonialism. These legacies in turn structure the relationship between the racialized postcolonial state and its oppressed groups.

Many African countries have indeed experienced some forms of democratic transitions during the 1980s and 1990s.[3] However, these political transitions have managed in different contexts to provide neither a lasting peace nor a sustainable democracy. Contemporary African experiences of political democratization have shown that the consolidation of political democracy cannot be achieved without addressing the legacies of the past. In the Sudan, confronting the legacies of discrimination, racism, and social prejudice is perquisite for any attempt to forge a conducive environment for sustainable political and economic development.

Contemporary political experiences in the Sudan suggest that although crucial, political democracy is not necessarily enough—in the context of contested histories and identities—to secure and maintain the civil rights of citizenship or to sustain a democratic rule of law. Civil rights of citizenship have always been violated in the Sudan during so-called democratic periods. Without securing the civil rights of all citizens, the realization of democratic citizenship is unfulfilled. The history and nature of the state in contemporary Africa is deeply embedded in the colonial foundation. Colonial rule institutionalized ethnic and racial entitlements, rights, and privileges, and thus created unequal forms of citizenship.

This colonial construct, as SaidAdjumobi argues,

> [D]e-individualizes citizenship and makes it more of a group or community entitlement. Rather than the state providing a common bond for the people through the tie of citizenship, with equal rights, privileges, and obligations, both in percepts and practice, people's loyalties are bifurcated.[4]

As a result, ethnic and racial community, rather than citizenship, becomes the basis for political and economic entitlements. The result is usually tension and the escalation of political violence in the postcolonial state as claims of marginalization, exclusion, and domination among individuals and groups are experienced.

Of course, the development of new democracies in Africa usually differs from Western experiences. It is not only that their different histories and identities necessarily require a different discourse to understand its historical specificity in diverse cultural settings. It is also that these histories suggest the need to question and problematize the conventional perceptions about democratization and peace in multiethnic and cultural contexts. In the Sudan, democratic political system shows, for example, both the incapability of democratic elections for realizing democratic citizenship, and the inability of a democratic discourse based on elections for understanding the challenges of existing competing visions of histories and identities in the country. Previous democratic experiences in the Sudan, for instance, have shown that violence, injustice, and impunity were common.[5] Consequently, the ruling groups embarked on a project of undermining many institutions of law and justice leading to the abuse of power by police and the military, the brutalization of politically marginalized groups, the obstruction of the principle of legality, and an unequal distribution of citizens' rights. For instance, the imposition of the *Sharia* (Islamic laws) in 1983, and the policy of

Arabization in the Sudan in general have relegated people of the Southern Sudan to the status of subjects rather than citizens.

Therefore, the conventional understanding of political democracy, which underscores the civil element of citizenship and its constitutional elements of justice and law in the daily lives of citizens, certainly in Africa, overlooks these fundamental historical concerns. In the Sudan, where the state legally reinforced discrimination, the unintended result was major political violence between those who ruled through the mechanism of exclusion and those who demanded either inclusion in the state, or the exercise of right of self-determination. These historical and political circumstances have shown the difficulty of consolidating the project of inclusive nation-states in societies where a single vision of history and identity has been imposed over diverse ethnic and cultural communities.

In the Sudan, the politics of history and identity has become closely associated with state power. The use and abuse of history is a very common practice in the Sudan. For instance, the contemporary rise of Islamism and Arabism, crystallized by the consolidation of power by the National Islamic Front (NIF) in the Sudan, has been predicated upon a rewriting of Sudanese history, and the utilization of particular historical narratives to lay claim to a single unified national identity: the Arab identity.

There are two contested strands to this identity, one is the contemporary political ideology, and the intentions of mobilizing politically by using the slogan of religion, in this case the slogan of Islam. In the case of the Sudan, the central claim is that Sudanese identity must by necessity be an Arab/Islamic identity. The proponents claim that there has to be an Arab/Islamic linear identity from the very foundation of Sudanese history up to the present.[6] Only a historically linear identity appears to give historical legitimization to what is being done and said in the name of Islam and Arabism today, while it excludes other groups that are considered non-Arabs and non-Muslims. The other strand relates to the Southern Sudanese elites' use of history and their endorsement of a colonial nineteenth-century historiography. Southern elites have unquestioningly accepted the theories and categories of colonial writers about the past, projecting a precolonial period of about a thousand years in which Sudan's history was dominated by two monolithic, antagonistic religious and racial communities— the Arab and the African. The contradiction is that the southern discourse claims that it is returning to a precolonial understanding of Sudanese history, whereas in fact the essential formulations are rooted in colonial historiography.[7] There is a tendency to go back to nineteenth-century ideas and of course, basically, those are ideas that fit in with the colonial and the dominant Northern Sudanese discourse of Arabism and Islamism. In this discourse, the Sudanese civilization has been perceived as a purely Islamic civilization, and the African contribution as being negative.

The Racialized State and Construction of "National History"

Through history, Arabs and Europeans have written so much about the people of the Sudan. In their writings, people of the Sudan were presented to the outside world as two different regional and racial categories in terms of history and culture.[8] The northern region of the Sudan has been perceived as "oriental" while the southern region has been considered as "inhabited by people without history." As a result, the Northern Sudanese have been labeled as Arab, "Muslims," and "civilized," whereas Southern Sudanese as "black," "heathen," and "primitive." This mode of thinking is also linked closely with the elitist and racist views of the dominant groups. Since then, not only history and identity became linked to the process of state formation in the precolonial period, but were also used as a source of contested nationalism in the colonial and postcolonial periods. Contemporary academic discourse on the Sudan has been influenced by the colonial discourse on Africa.[9] This discourse is only interested in studying the institutions of the centralized state and its ruling groups. Consequently, the history of those who were subjugated by the state has been either ignored or misrepresented.

History is seen, in many postcolonial African states as a means for nation-building. In the Sudan, for instance, shortly after independence in 1956, the postcolonial state embarked on the reconstruction of "national history." Precolonial "heroes" and nationalist leaders (mainly Arabized and Islamized) were reinvented as the embodiment of "national essence," and used to encourage the belief that Sudanese had shared historical experiences. In the Sudanese context, history has never been about the past, but about the present contested realities. The past was misrepresented purposely in a way that served the present purposes: the legitimacy of the racialized state.

If one changes the focus of analysis from the linear narrative of history to the construction and nature of state formation in the Sudan, one comes up with a series of historical questions that are much more meaningful for understanding the contemporary political violence in the country. These questions have to do with social contestation, social assimilation, incorporation, hierarchy, and power. These questions are not the kind of issues that the dominant historical narrative addresses. The presentation of Arab past, as great golden ages, becomes absurd and meaningless.

It is true that history is not given, but constructed. This, in part, explains why historical reconstruction is essential if we seek to understand the crisis of the postcolonial state in Africa. During the colonial era, it would be expected that the history of the colonized, which was written by the colonizers and considered the official "truth" would project the vision and discourse of the colonizing powers: their biases and their deliberate misrepresentations of the colonized. The postcolonial state, however, has reproduced the invented colonial discourse on Africa to legitimize its power over diverse peoples and histories. History instead has become a major site for identity-formation in the postcolonial context.

Examining the processes of construction and the nature of the state is important to the understanding of the root causes of conflicts. Contemporary studies on identities and conflicts are concerned with the construction of identities, and with the relationship of these identities to history and the processes of state formation.[10] The focus is not only on how the past has led to the present, but also how history is used or created. This perspective certainly enables us to reconsider the conventional wisdom that tends to perceive identities as unchangeable realities. It also enables us to distinguish between the myth of genealogies and history.

The official narrative of history in the Sudan has created a particular discourse and vision of the past. The dominant ruling groups in the Sudan have systematically used history to provide justification and legitimacy for their own power. In reality, however, the country contains multiple identities and histories, which reflect the historical realities and experiences of their people.[11] Like other African countries, the Sudan is the land for a clash of nationalist discourses that offer competing narratives of the past and contemporary forms of identity, constructing the Sudan in different forms. Northern-based nationalism in the Sudan has created, for itself, a genealogy that stretches into the Islamic Arab past and suggests a primordial and essential identity shared by all those who reside within the Northern Sudan, regardless of their particular ethnic, racial, and cultural orientations.

Consequently, the culture of the Arabized Northern Sudanese and the Islamization have been presented as the unifying genius of the Sudan bringing together diverse "primitive" tribal groups within common identity through the mechanisms of Arabization and Islamization. In this sense, Arabization and Islamization became sanctioned by state policy. The subordinated groups certainly resisted these new imposed "national identity." Other discourses of national identity, however, challenge this view, and insist that these united national identities are in reality expressions of Arab chauvinisms. The Southern Sudanese, for instance, have rejected the imposed vision of national identity and instead have asserted their own narratives of national identity. This new discourse emphasizes the importance of the indigenous cultural practices and its distinctiveness.

Given the history of forced population movement in the country, none of the main ethnic or linguistic groups are racially or historically homogeneous. Anyone with close knowledge of the culture, social organization, and recorded history of any of the supposedly homogenous groups in the Sudan will know that their origins are in fact heterogeneous and that any notions of common descent are mythical. Indeed, a shared and distinctive language, religion, and custom, are the products, not of generations of isolation from others, but of processes of assimilation, negotiation, accommodation, and conquest and social construction, in a context of power relations with the state and with competing visions of histories and identities.

In the Sudan, history has always been associated with the institution of the state and the ruling elites. Thus, the production of the national history by the state has become a vehicle for nation-building and state-building. The power of the state is closely involved in this history, and it does not guarantee even a provisional truth. Therefore, in the case of the Sudan, we have to distinguish between two types of history: official history, which tends to be institutionalized by state policy, and the subaltern histories of those who are excluded from the state. While the former consolidates and justifies the existing nation-state, the latter seeks to question its legitimacy by reconstructing and reinterpreting the subaltern.

The official history however has conditioned the truth of the Arab Islamic regime in the Sudan. History as a knowledge system, of course, is firmly rooted in institutional practices that invoke the nation-state. For instance, scholars have examined the manner in which the discourses of nationalism are constructed as hegemonic, which attempt to forge a collective will and establish popular identification with the "imagined political community" of the nation.[12] Disseminated through state institutions, such as schools, political parties, the bureaucracy, and the communication industry, national discourses perceive the people as national subjects and aim to incorporate diverse people and heritages into a totalizing national project.[13]

Such official discourses provide particular constructions of the national past, which work to produce a consensus about the past and to ratify the rule of existing regimes. Moreover, within the imaginary unity of the nation, differences based on race, class, gender, and regional distinctions disappear and are overridden by the symbolic oneness of the people-nation.[14] Such hegemonic discourses often appropriate certain local traditions and reinvent them as natural, while dismissing other traditions that pose too great a threat to the reproduction of the existing sociopolitical order. In such a context, invented traditions may also be employed to function as identification with the national.[15] The meta-narrative in the Sudan is a selective representation of the past that has been an integral part of the ideology of the dominant ruling elites. This discourse can be also seen as an expansion of the state ideology about the historical right of Arabized Islamized peoples to rule over non-Muslim and non-Arab groups.

The history of slavery and violence has been treated in the colonial and postcolonial discourse of contemporary Sudan as an aberration, in the sense that violence is seen as something removed from the general run of precolonial and colonial history of the Sudan: an exceptional moment, not the real history of the

Sudan at all. The history of violence however cannot be excluded from the historical processes of state formation in the region. It is this violence that plays a decisive role in the establishment of meaning, in the creation of truth regimes, and in deciding whose grand narrative wins.

In the context of the Sudan, the historical boundaries of the state were perceived in religious and racial terms. Islam and Arabism were considered the carriers of civilization and those who lived outside these boundaries were inevitable target of subordination, exploitation, and enslavement. The Islamic and Arabized orientations of the state also enhanced and justified the economic exploitation of internal resources, and laid the foundation for the related notion of subjugated peoples and their resources as disposable entities. In the Sudan, as the state grew economically and ideologically, both its internal and external boundaries became the cultural and political divide between "civilization" and "savagery," the ideological marker between law and the absence of law within the Islamic realm.

Thus, the formation and reproduction of identities, whether they are personal, communal, or national, involve some sort of a making of history. Therefore, the official history is often born out of the expanding power of the state, which justifies its coercion and hegemony over those who are conquered and subjugated through the process of state formation. Understanding the relationship among history, identity, and conflict in the Sudan, thus requires the acknowledgment of the multitude of levels of history. In the Sudan, there is not one history, but many. This understanding is very useful in the context of political violence for it locates both the precolonial and the colonial periods in the postcolonial history and identifies the continuous as well as the discontinuous factors and their interplay in the contemporary political violence and its relation to the crisis of postcolonial citizenship in the Sudan.

Citizenship and Postcolonial State
in the Sudan

The competing visions of identities and histories, which are produced through the processes of state formation, posed serious challenges to the notion of citizenship in the postcolonial period. The marginalized groups have challenged the dominant racial and political identities. Indeed, the recent debate on citizen and subject in African Studies is very significant for understanding the root causes of the civil wars and political conflicts in the region.[16] This debate offers new theoretical alternative that enables us to investigate the relationship between the process of state formation and the production of political or racial identities and their association with various levels of entitlements in the postcolonial period.

Indeed, the concept of nation-state cannot be meaningful without the notion of citizenship. However, throughout history, the Sudan has had two categories of populations: citizens and subjects. The state was involved in the processes of incorporating peoples of southern region into its boundary forcefully. Consequently, the manner in which the process of state formation was carried out has had a significant impact on the definition and the meaning of citizenship in the postcolonial nation-state in the Sudan. Citizenship, thus, is an instrument of social and political closure through which the state lays claim to and defines its sovereignty, authority, legitimacy, and identity. However, in the African contexts, the processes of state formation have shaped the nature and the meaning of citizenship. The question is, then, how did this dichotomy evolve and what are its implications for the postcolonial state, identities, and politics in Africa?

The colonial political system was predicated on the logic of dualism, of institutional and territorial segregation, and laws that Mamdani described as a "bifurcated state" or the logic of decentralized despotism. On the one hand, there was the central state governed by civil laws, which was the domain of the colonizers, basically urban based, and on the other hand, there was the local state or the native authorities, which enforced customary laws. The former was the domain of rights and privileges associated with citizenship; the latter was the domain of culture and custom. The natives or the colonized were subjects and therefore not entitled to citizenship rights or benefits. The agency of the local state and native authority rule was the chiefs. In the chiefs were vested administrative, executive, legislative, extractive, and judicial powers. The chief was the law. Therefore, while civil law was racialized, customary law was ethnicized.[17]

These historical circumstances thus have come to problematize the notion of citizenship and democratization in postcolonial Africa. In the Sudan, the colonial policy of indirect rule has had tremendous consequences in legalizing the existence of two competing political identities: African versus Arab identities. These historical circumstances indeed influenced the mentality and the manner in which the anticolonial nationalists came to define and understand the identity of the postcolonial state. Like many African countries, the anticolonial nationalism in the Sudan failed to transcend the colonial legalized racial and ethnic differences. Instead, the Northern-based nationalist movement used Arabism and Islamism as pillars of the postcolonial state in the Sudan.

If Arab and African identities resulted from the practice of enslavement during the precolonial period, the colonial state, however, gave it a new legal dimension by institutionalizing these racialized identities through colonial polices of indirect rule. African and Arab thus were transformed from flexible cultural identities to rigid political identities through the state policies. In addition, the very category African was legally dismantled as different groups of "natives" were set apart on the basis of ethnicity.

From this perspective, thus, both race and ethnicity need to be seen as political and not cultural. Although these political identities embody cultural meaning, their production was a result of how power was being used in the context of the state formation. In his recent study on the Sudan's civil wars, Douglas Johnson argues,

> The origins of the Sudan's current problem predate the unequal legacy of the colonial system in the twentieth century. They can be found in the ideas of legitimate power and governance developed in the Sudanic states of the eighteenth and nineteenth centuries, which were incorporated into the structures of the Turco-Egyptian empire, achieved new force in the jihad state of the Mahdiyya, and were never fully replaced, but rather . . . occasionally adapted by the twentieth century colonial state.[18]

Indeed, the colonial state constructed segregated institutional system of rule in Africa. However, the colonial project cannot be held solely responsible for the creation of racial and political identities in Africa. The history of the precolonial African societies also needs to be examined carefully so that we can come to grips with its impacts. In the Sudan, for instance, the legacy of enslavement during the precolonial period has had serious consequences in the colonial and the postcolonial periods. The violent political conflicts in southern and western regions of the Sudan are manifestations of legacies of the past, namely slavery and colonialism. These legacies in turn structure the political, economic, and cultural relationships between the postcolonial state and its oppressed groups. Indeed, the experience of slavery continues to mark the people of the southern and the western Sudan, for instance, because the constructed ideological perceptions of difference and hierarchy created by slavery and institutionalized by colonial policies have been maintained by the racialized postcolonial state. The implication of these historical and political processes is felt in the present political violence in the country. This alternative theoretical perspective would certainly enable us to understand how people who were not previously described as "races" have come to be described in these racial terms; and how these historical circumstances have become a source of political violence in the postcolonial period.

CHAPTER 2

SLAVERY, COLONIALISM, AND STATE FORMATION IN THE SUDAN

Neither culture nor race is at the heart of the current conflict in the Sudan. Rather it is the racialized state that transformed cultural identities into political identities through the practice of slavery in the precolonial period, indirect rule during the colonial period, and state exclusive policy of citizenship in the postcolonial period. The goal here is to examine how these political and racial identities have been constructed through the process of state formation.

I will begin first by raising some historical questions related to this study. Is the Sudan really divided into two regions with two different racial and religious compositions? What do African and Arab mean in the Sudanese context? Are they racial, cultural, or political identities? Do they have history and politics? We are often told that British colonialism divided the country into two separate regions and invented an African identity in the South. But we are not told that colonialism also fragmented the African identity into ethnicities through the policy of indirect rule in the Southern Sudan. Indeed, this policy transformed flexible cultural communities into conflicting political entities. The current civil war and the spread of political violence in the Sudan cannot be understood without recognizing the legacies of slavery and colonialism.

Slavery, Race, and State Formation

In the scholarship on African slavery, we are told that in Muslim societies, the enslaved person was often not treated as property and that she/he was more valued as a member of the family. Yet slaves in Africa were not treated much differently from those in the "New World." The descendants of a slave were also slaves until freed by the master. Similarly, the castration of young males to prevent procreation with "noble" females, particularly married wives of the nobility, resembles the cruelty of New World slavery.

Indeed, when the West was in the process of abolishing the institution of slavery, the Arab and African leaders, especially in the Central Sudan and northeast Africa, were increasing their own traffic in human beings on the premise that the *Sharia*, or the Islamic law, allowed the enslavement of non-Muslims. By 1888, when the last state, Brazil, abolished slavery, northeast Africa and the Central Sudan witnessed an increase in the number of slaves taken out of their communities by Arab traders and Islamicized local leaders to be sold in central African markets, in Egypt, the Middle East, and in the Ottoman Empire. In the state of Bornu, for instance, Louis Brenner argues "such raids were legitimate in the eyes of the Bornu leaders, since, according to Islamic law, the Muslim state is in a perpetual state of war with the countries of the unbelievers, who are legally enslavable."[1] Mohamad Ibn Al Tunisi, a Muslim leader, argues, however, that Islamic law, although justifying war and enslavement, prescribed that "infidels" be allowed to choose between war and tribute, and between peaceful and forced conversion. He further stated:

> According to the Divine world itself, war is the legitimate and holy means to bring men under the yoke of religion; for as soon as the infidels feel the arms of Islam, and see their power humiliated, and their families led away into slavery, they will desire to enter into the right way, in order to preserve their persons and goods.

However, before restoring to the extreme means, we must invite them to submit to the laws of Islam, and warn them many times of the misfortunes they will bring upon themselves by their incredulity . . . if they take up arms against you, whoever is made captive shall be sold.[2]

During the nineteenth century, the ruling group monopolized Sudan's slave trade, which became its most important export commodity eclipsing ivory and gold. Bahr al Ghazal, for instance, became an increasingly active slave trading region during the late 1890s, when parts of the Southern Sudan "ran dry of anybody worth enslaving," according to Robert Collins.[3] Indeed, the need of the court and those of the various palaces of the nobility, and a large class of aristocrats who refused to work, made the slave trade and slavery essential to economic and political stability of the society. In Sinnar kingdom, for example, farming and slave ownership made the merchant class wealthy.

> Even the most modest owned field hands to cultivate the holdings and girls to carry water and grind grain, while the leading merchants had large slave establishments. The major slaveholders often sent their family slaves to work as prostitutes in towns along the trade routes; the girls were given living quarters, but paid a fixed monthly fee from their earnings to the master. This practice existed also among the nobility but it was unknown "in the more traditional and commercially isolated populations in the Southern provinces."[4]

The economic impact of the slave trade and slavery was certainly great in Africa. Without it, the slaving states and empires could not function or survive. Indeed, as Cordell argues,

> Slave raiding . . . allowed the mobilization of labor on a large scale than previously possible, accompanied by, appropriation of a great part of its product. The small-scale household labor force characteristic of indigenous non-Muslim societies was not eliminated, but it

became a component of a multifaceted system of forced labor that also included plantation production. The perpetuation of this system depended in part on continued access to firearms, powder, and other long-distance trade goods from the north which could be obtained only in exchange for slaves and ivory.[5]

The region of northeast Africa, and the Sudan in particular, can be characterized in the eighteenth and nineteenth centuries as a frontier war zone, where the primary role of the state was to wage war and raid the surrounding communities using all means at its disposal.[6] Besides territorial conquest as one of the objectives for violence, the main incentive for warring in northeast Africa was the acquisition of slaves. In the Sudan, for instance, there would have been fewer wars had slavery and the slave trade not been the main feature of state expansion, which in the name of *Allah*— God—authorized the "faithful" to enslave those who were non-Muslim.

In the Sudan the processes of enslavement have their roots in the precolonial period. For over four hundred years, enslavement and state expansion transformed cultural differences between various groups into political differences. In AD 1504, an Arabized and Islamized group founded the Funj kingdom in Central Sudan by overthrowing the kingdom of Christian Nubia. For the Arabized and Islamized group, this new kingdom had "become a guarantee of peace and order,"[7] and for the majority of non-Arab and non-Muslim groups it became the tool of destruction. The Funj kingdom not only laid the foundation of a racialized state but it also reinvented a new identity for the Sudan. The newcomers introduced their new system of racialized politics and religion. Between 1504 and 1820, this kingdom institutionalized Islam and developed it into the official religion of the kingdom.[8]

The Arabization and Islamization of the Northern and the Central Sudan in the sixteenth and seventeenth centuries, enabled many groups in the north to produce genealogies that linked their families to Arab origins.[9] Between the sixteenth and seventeenth centuries, the Islamized Funj and Darfur kingdoms ruled the northern regions of the Sudan. According to Douglas Johnson:

> Sennar [Funj], established along the Blue Nile in the sixteenth century AD, raided the Ethiopian foothills, the Nuba mountains, and the White Nile plains. The Darfur Sultanate, established in the western Sudan in the seventeenth century AD, raided mainly to the south in Dar Fartit, or what is now Western Bahr al Ghazal. This remained the hunting ground for hands radiating out of Darfur well into the twentieth century.[10]

The societies of these two kingdoms were divided into three social groups: the nobility, their subjects, and slaves.[11] Social relationships between the nobility and the subjects were based on subordination. This form of social structure was maintained by customary laws and was reflected in property ownership, legal rights, and marriage forms. While the noble group controlled political and economic power, the subjects provided labor and paid tribute.[12] Slave institutions, however, were more effective among riverian Muslim societies of the Northern Sudan than among others such as the Fur. In the Northern and the Central Sudan, to own land was a prerequisite to independence, integrity, and social status, but to perform menial labor precluded all three. The route to higher social status was to relieve oneself of performing menial labor even on one's own land. Performing agricultural labor for someone else was socially humiliating.[13] Consequently, slaves became crucial in performing agricultural activities, and Arabic-speaking riverian Muslims of the Sudan came to consider their cultural norms and values as being superior to those of the non-Muslim and Arab groups.

Being a Muslim in these societies, however, did not protect many Muslims from being enslaved. In the Sudan, captives included many Muslim from western Africa and the Western

Sudan. Slaves were usually obtained through organized raids on the non-Muslim/non-Arab population in the Southern Sudan and the Nuba Mountains.[14] Indeed, a racialized society like the Northern Sudan provided a social justification for those who practiced slavery.[15] Slaves were also drafted into the army. Surplus slaves, however, were exported and provided a major source of wealth for the ruling class in both kingdoms. With the increased demand for slaves in the late eighteenth century, the southern regions of these kingdoms were transformed into slave-raiding regions with a complex pattern of racialized interactions between Arab and non-Arab groups. Ideological and racial categories were constructed or invented along these frontiers. Muslims in the north, for example, claimed for themselves patrilineal descent from distinguished Arab ancestors.[16] This "conventional acceptance of the claim to be Arab was of crucial importance,"[17] for it demarcated and racialized the people of the Sudan. Color in itself became quite irrelevant; many Arab Sudanese were and are darker than some peoples in the south.[18] But descent did matter; even conversion to Islam could not fully compensate for the absence of an accepted Arab ancestry. When Southerners converted to Islam, their immediate descendants were still not fully accepted as equals into the Northern Sudanese society, either politically or socially.

During the nineteenth century, the region of northeast Africa underwent profound economic, political, and social changes. The superpower of the region, the Ottoman Empire, was in a state of decline and disintegration. Both Britain and France struggled to take control of Egypt and the Red Sea. The first encounter between two Western powers occurred when France invaded Egypt in 1798. However, in 1801, France was forced to end its occupation of Egypt, and Mohammed Ali Pasha established his rule there. Mohammed Ali Pasha invaded the Sudan in 1821 in search of slaves, ivory, and gold in order to finance his Egyptian project of modernization. The Turko-Egyptian conquest laid the basis of a centralized state in Northern Sudan. Although the Turko-Egyptian state introduced modern innovations such as schools, the telegraph, and a railway in the Sudan, it also embarked on the enslavement of people of the southern region and used their labor on cotton plantations and for irrigation schemes. Douglas Johnson stated:

> The new rulers [Turko-Egyptian] in the Sudan continued official slave raids on a massive scale, and imposed a tribute in slaves upon their new subjects. Collaboration in slave-raids into non-Muslim territories thus became a virtual duty for some of the Muslim pastoralists in the Sudan. The Shaiqiyya from north of Khartoum, the Rufa'a of the Blue Nile, and the Baqqara along the White Nile and in the west soon were involved in official raids with the army, or were organizing raids of their own.[19]

From 1821 to 1831, the Turko-Egyptian government began a new stage of state-organized slave raids, which first targeted people in Ethiopia and the Nuba Mountains. The collapse of the ivory market and the practical difficulties of establishing a stable trading system in other commodities, however, encouraged many merchants from the north to turn to the slave trade as the only viable economic activity.[20] As a result, slaves were turned into a means of payment for the local agents and soldiers of the slave traders or the slave hunters. During the Turko-Egyptian rule, not only did the number of slaves increase but domestic slavery too became more common in the Northern Sudan. The army stationed along the Abyssinian frontier looted the highlands for food and supplies with impunity. Traders used slaves to pay tribute to the government in slaves. Peasants in the north began earning their income by sending at least one member of their household to the slave trade. However, Egypt's expansion to the Sudan looking for slaves and mineral wealth and its desire to control the source of Nile brought Egypt into conflict with Abyssinians of the Gondor area.

By 1860, powerful regional rulers with their own slaves and private slave armies under their command were established in the Southern Sudan and the areas bordering Ethiopia. It was not uncommon for slaves to be captured by an army composed of slaves. The practice of enslavement during the process of state formation has also contributed to the intensification of racial boundaries. According to Douglas Johnson:

> During the Turkiyya the slave population in the north was drawn very largely from the southern Sudan, and in the popular mind slaves and "blacks" were synonymous. Even southern Sudanese who became Muslims or exercised some power in the colonial society—as those in the army certainly did—were stigmatized by their slave status or slave origins.[21]

The demand for slaves increased with the pace of the economic development process in Egypt, as the demand for labor grew higher. Egyptians then turned to slaves from Abyssinia and its southern region to replace the Egyptian rural labor force, while practically all households living in major towns had at least one slave working as a domestic servant. In 1876, Sir Samuel Baker reported that "every household in Upper Egypt in the Delta was dependent upon slave-services . . . in fact, Egyptian society without slaves was like a carriage devoid of wheels; it could not proceed."[22]

Slave exports to the Middle East from the ports of Massawa and Swakin added importance to the value of slavery and the slave trade in the region. All this encouraged a large number of northern peasants in the Sudan to abandon their rural work and engage in slavery and the slave trade.[23] Consequently, traders from the Arab world expanded their penetration of Abyssinia. Wealth obtained from these activities was used to purchase modern arms and for further subjugation of other groups, which negatively impacted politics and society.

Brutal slave raiding, corruption, and economic exploitation, therefore, characterized the period of Turko-Egyptian rule in the Sudan. Ironically, as the official slave trade under Turko-Egyptian rule came to an end in 1877, a new pro-slavery and pro–slave trade state emerged to take its place in the Sudan. These circumstances allowed the Mahdist movement of 1885–1898 to gain popular support and finally defeat Turko-Egyptian rule. After the outbreak of the Mahdist revolt, the majority of Turkish, European, and other foreign merchants and slave traders were forced to leave the south in the hands of traders from the north, the so-called *jallaba*.[24] Although these slave traders emerged from a number of distinct Arabized groups, they described themselves as members of an imagined single Arab community.

Indeed, "conversion of non-Arab slaves after conquest was no sanctuary from the servile conditions."[25] Even after their conversion, they were still considered to be second-class Muslims because they were not Arab, based on their race and descent. According to Asafa Jalata, embracing Orthodox Christianity or Islam did not change the status of the subjugated people in northeast Africa. He further argues:

> Blackness has been associated with a doon in Somalia, Bariya or Galla or Shanqilla in Ethiopia, and abd in Sudan. Since Blackness is the metaphor of powerlessness in these countries, it does not matter if the skin color of politically dominant and subjugated peoples is black today. Although the indigenous Africans phenotypically transformed the descendants of Arab immigrants, the Africanized ethnonations have racialized the indigenous Africans by converging religion, identity, and power in order to dominate and exploit them.[26]

At the ideological level, the slaving area was constructed by those involved in the slave trade in terms of Islamic versus non-Islamic, Arab versus non-Arab descent, brown versus black color, with each racial category giving meaning and representation to its opposite. These invented categories included terms such as *abd* or slave for Southerners or *Fallata* or *Gharaba* for western African immigrants and Western Sudanese.[27] Consequently, the importance of race in the Sudan is linked with the construction of Arab origin. Thus, with the creation of these categories during the process of state formation, the people of the Southern Sudan, the Nuba Mountains, and the Upper Blue Nile became prey for northern Muslim slave traders. Janet J. Ewald, in her book *Soldiers, Traders and Slaves*, described this process:

> Muslim masters referred to all local people who did not practice Islam as abid (slaves) even if these southerners had not been enslaved by force. Flags bearing Quranic verses flew over traders, soldiers, and slaves when they marched in caravans.[28]

The slave trade during the Mahdist period led to a clash of racialized identities out of which emerged a violent political regime in which the people of the south were subjected to discrimination and exploitation.[29] These precolonial processes of enslavement, indeed, imposed social meanings on social, cultural, and religious differences among the people of the Sudan and served as the basis for the structuring of society.

Colonialism and the Legacy of Slavery (1898–1947)

Labor Policies

When the British colonized the Sudan in 1898, they were faced with two fundamental concerns—the problem of slavery and the need for law and order in the Southern Sudan. Informed by the colonial discourse on Africa, the British administrators introduced new policies for labor control and indirect rule in the Southern Sudan. Peter McLoughlin has estimated that 20 to 30 percent of the population in Northern Sudan at the time of Anglo-Egyptian conquest in 1898 were slaves.[30] As I argued earlier, since the nineteenth century, the cultural fabric of the society was imagined by the dominant ruling groups to be Arab-Islamic. Those who did not belong to this imagined identity were considered enslaveable.

The defeat of the Mahdist state by the Anglo-Egyptian forces in 1898, however, did not change the social and economic reality of the Northern Sudan. The new colonial power did not challenge and delegitimize the institution of slavery and the slave trade in the Sudan. Rather, the process of consolidating the colonial state formation forced the British administrators to tolerate it and work closely with the slave traders for several decades. Despite the British moral discourse of antislavery, the practice continued in the Sudan for decades.[31] The colonial policy was to end slavery in the Sudan, but in such a way so as not to challenge the power of the Northern Sudanese slave traders. Lord Kitchener, the first governor-general of the Anglo-Egyptian Sudan, declared the policy of his government on slavery as follows:

> Slavery is not recognized in the Sudan, but as long as service is willingly rendered by servants to masters it is unnecessary to interfere in the conditions existing between them. Where, however, any individual is subjected to cruel treatment and his or her liberty interfered with, the accused can be tried on such charges, which are offences against the law, and in serious cases of cruelty the severest sentences should be imposed.[32]

In order to avoid a renaissance of Mahdism, the colonial state indeed tolerated existing practices of domination including slavery. By reason of this policy a particular version of political identities was maintained and utilized in which people in the Sudan were divided into categories in terms of rights: enslaveable and freemen, non-Arab and Arab.[33] One of the main factors that

contributed to the continuation of slavery was British administrators' attitudes toward Sudanese slavery.[34] They believed that sudden abolition would lead to moral decay and to social problems
such as vagrancy and prostitution. Of course, their perceptions
derived from the slave owners themselves, with whom administrators were closely associated. However, these views were used to
advance the economic interests of the colonial state and the traditional religious and tribal leaders. As C.A. Willis, a senior British
administrator, remarked:

> The reactionary official takes his cue from the Arab, with whom
> he, as was pointed out above, is in closer touch than the slave. He
> likes order and discipline, and he wants to see production increase
> and habits of thrift and industry encouraged, and all these seem to
> be available under the system of domestic slavery.[35]

Sheikh Muddathir al Hajjaz, a leading religious figure, also
wrote:

> No slave should be allowed to leave his master before proving that
> he is badly treated by him. The government should take this line
> in dealing with slavery cases for at least seven years until the
> Sudanese prepare themselves gradually to the state of affairs they
> will have to fall into after the lapse of the slave period.[36]

The slow declining of slavery only occurred when wage labor
became available in the 1920s. The majority of this cheap labor
came from non-Arab groups such as western African immigrants.
The British government was convinced that a sudden death of
slavery would lead to economic collapse. For the purpose of
securing and maintaining labors for the British colonial economic
projects, the British divided the people of the Sudan legally into
three distinct racial categories: Arab, Sudanese for ex-slave, and
Fallata for western Africans. On the one hand, these categories

were based on the anthropological assumption that each group had certain qualities regarding labor; on the other hand, they were informed by the legacy of slavery.

The Policy of Indirect Rule in Southern Sudan (1930–1947)

A key element of the colonial discourse on Africa was the characterization of Africans as "primitive." Christian Britain perceived itself to be morally superior to "heathen" Africa, reinforced by theories of racial hierarchy. In reference to the Southern Sudan, John Howell argues that British administrators, motivated by a sense of Victorian nationalism,

> Saw the South Sudan as an area devastated by the nineteenth century slave trade from the North: thus the re-creation of a stable political order would depend on the restoration of a discipline and authority which many tribes appeared to have lost in the decades of ravage and plunder. It seemed only logical therefore that northern . . . influence should be eliminated from the South while this hoped for tribal renaissance took place.[37]

In 1898, a joint Anglo-Egyptian force under Kitchener defeated the Mahdists at the battle of Omdurman and took control of the Northern Sudan. Condominium rule in the Sudan began with the conclusion, on January 19, 1899, of an agreement between the British government and the government of the Khedive of Egypt.[38] When the British came to the Sudan, they reproduced racialized identities. Consequently, the Sudan was divided into two supposed regions—Arab North and African South. The British administration accepted the racialized ideology of the nineteenth century that the south was inferior to the north and Muslim people were civilized, while non-Muslim were not. According to J. Winder, a British officer, "the north possesses ethical foundations of a society, and the south does not." He further claimed that:

> In the north, Islam controlled the lives and habits of the people, consequently an administrator, once having learnt the basic features of Islam, had the key to understanding the society he worked in. In the south there was no such basis. There was no common ethic foundation to assist the administrator to an understanding of his people. Further, in the north, sharia law governed personal behaviour . . . the people were used to a body of law. In the south tribal custom differed from one people to another; no single code of behaviour was recognized.[39]

The British aim in occupying the south was to control the Nile Valley, but the problem that faced the colonial state after colonizing the south was how to rule the people of the South Sudan. The early objective of the colonial rule was to continue the centralizing policies of the Turko-Egyptian and Mahdist regimes. In order to deal with the problem in the Sudan the administration had implemented a strategy of so-called native administration, meaning the separation of one ethnic group from another so as to avoid conflict. According to Kitchener, tribal policy was intended "to seek out the better class of native, through whom we may hope to influence the whole population."[40]

The strong resistance of the Southern Sudanese forced the British to change the policy of centralized administration in the Sudan. In 1920, after two decades of centralized administration and growing Southern Sudanese resistance, the Milner Mission recommended a decentralized system.

> Having regard to its vast extent and the varied character of its inhabitants, the administration of its different parts should be left as far as possible in the hands of the native authorities, where they exist, under British supervision. . . . Decentralization and

employment, wherever possible, of native agencies for the simple administrative needs of the country in its present stage of development, would make both for economy and efficiency.[41]

Indirect rule was introduced to the Sudan in 1921. Daly argued that indirect rule came to the Sudan as a result of two unrelated events: the dissemination of Lord Lugard's *The Dual Mandate in British Tropical Africa* (1922), and the arrival of Sir John Maffey as governor general in 1926.[42] C.L. Temple defined indirect rule as "a system which leaves in existence the administrative machinery which had been created by the natives themselves . . ."[43] This meant governing through existing political and social structures and the use of tribal chiefs or *sheikh* as agents of the colonial power. According to MacMichael,

> It is of vital importance that we get the best men to be sheikhs if we are to expect them to exercise any authority and so gradually relieve the administrative staff of the Government of a proportion of its work. . . . the average Sheikh in many provinces is little better than a local scallywag deputed by the villages to do such things as the government require Sheikhs to do.[44]

He further claimed that a native

> Has his chief, secular or religious, and expects to have to obey him and to see authority upheld. To tell him that in the eyes of that curious phenomenon, the Law, all men are equal is merely to condemn the Law as an ass. . . . A sense of homage is natural to him. It is a good and sensible instinct, and it must be given scope.[45]

The method used in the selection of chiefs was contrary to existing practice according to which the chief must first be a spiritual leader and second a strong and respectable person. Instead, the British administrators chose common men or "white chiefs." Anthropologist Evans-Pritchard pointed out the difference between the government chiefs and the traditional ones:

> The functions of a native chief are to represent the unity of the tribe, maintained and expressed by warfare which he initiates; to store and distribute wealth, generally food, which he receives as tribute and dispenses in gifts and hospitality; to embody in his person the sanctity of law and custom, which are exacted in his name; and to be the symbol of his people's purpose and the pivot of their system of values. . . . A government chief, by contrast, acts as the bureaucratic agent of an alien administration. . . . He derives his authority not from tradition and the moral backing of his people, but the support of the government . . .[46]

For instance, Willis, governor of Upper Nile, was influenced by the "Hamitic" hypothesis and assumed that there was a chief among the Nuer who had been undermined by the Kujurs. Willis thus thought that by suppressing the Kujurs he could reinstate the chiefs. By 1928, Willis admitted that the idea of chief was itself invented by the government. In 1929, he was advocating the invention of the chief, but in the name of custom and tradition. In his letter, to the Civil Secretary, dated February 18, 1929, Willis explained his policy in the Upper Nile to the Civil Secretary:

> the growth of native administration by the development of tribal institutions and the strengthening of tribal customs and law, and in general to build up on native foundations . . . the building up of the a native administration on the foundations of tribal custom and organization is the only sound method of tackling these tribes, even to the point of inventing an organization where as with the Dinka, they have lost their own.[47]

As a consequence of this invented institution, the first step the government took was to cut off the south from the north through the promulgation of the Passports and Permits Ordinance in

October 1922, which empowered the governor general to declare any part of the Sudan a Closed District.[48] In the south, this new policy required the elimination of all the administrative officers who spoke Arabic in favor of local recruits from the missionary school. British administrators were to speak the local languages, or, if that was impossible, to speak English instead of Arabic.[49] In October 1922, Stack ordered that Bahr al-Ghazal, Mongalla, most of the Nuba Mountains and Upper Nile Provinces, and several other districts were to be

> closed districts to the extent that no person other than a native of the Sudan shall enter or remain therein unless he is the holder of a permit . . . to be obtained from the Civil secretary or from the Governor of the province . . . and that any native of the Sudan may be forbidden to enter or remain in the said districts by the Civil Secretary or the Governor of such provinces.[50]

Accordingly, no one would enter the closed region of the Southern Sudan without permission. The purpose of this policy was to eradicate Arab-Islamic influences, and to preserve the African identity of the south. On January 25, 1930, the Civil Secretary issued a directive to the governors of the three Southern Provinces of Upper Nile, Mongalla, and Bahr al Ghazal, with an accompanying memorandum. The directive stated

> The policy of the government in the southern Sudan is to build up series of self contained racial or tribal units with structures and organization based to whatever extent the requirement of equity and good government permits, upon indigenous customs, traditional usage and beliefs.[51]

The native rule not only denied the right of citizenship to the natives, but also transformed radically the social structures in the Southern Sudan, including the institution of the chief. Native authority rule and customary law under the colonial state meant the reinvention of what were traditional political institutions and what may be called customary laws in most precolonial societies in Africa. The colonial state ensured that there was no local regulatory check on the chief, who invented and reinvented what constitutes customary laws in line with the interests of the colonial authority. In Douglas Johnson's view,

> Not only did administrators discourage southern societies from "borrowing" their neighbours' customs, they also tried to interdict the imitation or adoption of Islamic customs and law. Native Administration thus encouraged indigenous religious diversity in the south, while in the north religious policy encouraged the tendency towards a greater uniformity of practice among Muslims.[52]

The selection of chiefs under the colonial rule was not based on any tradition or custom of the local people, but on the interest of the colonial administrators.[53] More importantly, by fragmenting the local people into native authorities with different sets of customary law or tribal laws, the colonial state constructed and invented ethnic identities, which were to plague the state later during the nationalist struggle and in the postcolonial period.

The British policy of the 1930s was to develop the Southern Sudan along "indigenous and African lines." This meant a return to tribal law and customs, tribal family life, and indigenous languages.[54] This policy legitimized the idea of the Southern Sudan as a "tribal-African" society. Accordingly, the mode of life of indigenous people was considered to be tied to these tribal and racial institutions. In practice, "chiefs" were created and legitimized to rule the people and to implement the government policies. Daly has pointed out:

> As it was articulated in the Sudan in the early 1920s, Indirect Rule meant the use of already established (and also, it was hoped, of long submerged) forms of indigenous political organization as a

means of governing. It was, in practice, as in its motivations, a method of maintaining an archaic diffusion of political power, a way to postpone or prevent homogenisation.[55]

The policy of indirect rule indeed had contributed to the fragmentation of the society along ethnic, regional, and tribal lines, and it prevented the possibility of forging a sense of national identity in the postcolonial period.

CHAPTER 3
NATIONALISM, STATE, AND IDENTITY POLITICS

As I have argued in chapter 2, the construction of racial, ethnic, and regional identities in the Sudan is inherently related to the process of state formation in the region. For instance, precolonial legacies of slavery and the policy of indirect rule during the colonial period have contributed to racialization and fragmentation of cultural societies into conflicting political ones. The nature and content of the process of state formation not only transformed sociopolitical structures of societies, but also conditioned the form of resistance and opposition to the colonial and the postcolonial state. In addition to creation and invention of political identities, the process of state formation during the colonial period had contributed to economic and political inequalities between various ethnic groups. Coupled with the persistence and the institutionalization of ethnic identity as a criterion for economic, social, and political entitlements, the realization of inclusive citizenship in the postcolonial period has become impossible, if not unattainable.

In Africa, the rise of competing visions of nationalism cannot be separated from the overall conflict over history and identity. In the sense that "the ways in which history is defined, imagined, and articulated is important in shaping competing visions of power and mobilization of ethnic identities within a particular power context."[1] Conflict over interpretations of history and identity of the postcolonial state has created competing visions of nationalism. In the case of the Sudan, the transition from colonialism to political independence marked the beginning of political conflict, which revolved around three fundamental issues: the political conflict over the identity of the postcolonial state, the status of the Southern Sudan in the postcolonial state, and conflict over the nature of the conflict. From its inception, the postcolonial state in the Sudan was besieged by a national identity crisis. The state officials claim the postcolonial state is Arab-Islamic state, while people of the Southern Sudan distance themselves from this state-pronounced identity. For both sides, history has become a source of different interpretations and justifications for political claims.

In fact, the history of nationalism in the Sudan has been the history of competing political claims over the identity of the postcolonial state rather than the struggle against European colonialism. As a result, leaders of various nationalist movements often have internalized the colonially created identities instead of transcending them. These nationalist movements reaffirm the racial barriers, which caused the political violence in the first place. During the colonial era, nationalist movements in the Sudan were socially constructed, with distinct regional, ethnic, class, and gender orientations, while others groups were excluded. This situation reflected the nature of the social and political structure that was emerging during the colonial period and of the polarization of societies along competing racial identities and regional lines. The excluded groups and regions were later subjected to systematic forms of state violence during the postcolonial period.

These historical and political circumstances certainly have led to political violence in the postcolonial period. However, the spread of political violence in contemporary Sudan should not be given, as is often done, cultural or racial interpretation.

David Apter argues thus:

> If we consider violence as a postmodern problematique, what is required to understand it is the interpretation of violence as a discourse and a semiotics, and a phenomenology in which violence is itself a mode of interpretation, with interpretation leading to violent events: protest, insurrection, terrorism.[2]

In the Sudan, nationalist groups have shared profoundly different visions of history and identity, each connecting past and present through different political interpretation. The conflicting interpretation of history and identity, however, cannot be understood without locating them within the historical processes of state formation. The history of precolonial Sudan was always recorded the ruling elites point of view, masked by glories of victory and conquest. However, the history of those who were enslaved and colonized have always either been excluded or misinterpreted. Those subjected to slavery were excluded, eliminated, or assimilated into the mainstream culture, thereby reinforcing the myth of a "unified state." The legacy of enslavement by the Northern Sudanese slave traders, however, has been deeply rooted in the Southern Sudanese political consciousness, making it difficult if not impossible for the central government to impose its authority in the south on the basis of a unitary political arrangement.

However, many nationalists believed that the political violence in the Sudan was a result of deep-seated, historically rooted ethnic hatreds. Some Southern nationalists, for instance, considered the Arab as an alien group to the society, and traceable to the invasion of Arabs from north Africa or Arabia. Consequently, the present conflicts are perceived as a carryover from the precolonial period of historical hatreds and antagonism, rooted in the attempt of Arabs to dominate Africans. For instance,

Dunstan M. Wai argued,

> The African collective memory of Arab participation in the slave trade and proselytization of Islam, more often by sword and through trade, produces a negative attitude towards Arabs. Africans perceive Arabs as cunning, crafty, dishonest, untrustworthy, and racially as well as culturally arrogant. Many Africans do not feel at ease in dealing with Arabs.[3]

Given this version of history, all attempts to forge sense of national identity guided by the principle of citizenship are doomed to fail. From this point of view, the postcolonial political violence are only the most recent and brutal manifestation of Arab efforts to impose their cultural and political hegemony in the face of African demands for full political participation. In the discourse of many Southerners, the precolonial and colonial history is invested with countless traces of extreme ethnic and racial oppression, thus yielding indisputable evidence of continuity between past and present. Indeed, in the Sudan, social and ethnic oppression was an established feature of the precolonial society, but these cycles of oppression and violence had taken different forms throughout the history of state formation. *The Southern Sudan Vision* stated:

> The people of southern Sudan are amongst the most politically oppressed and subjected people in the African continent, perhaps comparable only to the victims of the obnoxious apartheid system in South Africa. Their whole life history is nothing but a tragic catalogue of unprecedented suffering, indignities, massacres, slavery, racial and religious discrimination inflicted upon them by alien peoples and systems at varying phases of history.[4]

On the other hand, Northern Sudanese nationalists believe that the Arab-African crisis of identity is entirely the creation of the colonial power and bears no relationship whatsoever to the structure of the precolonial or postcolonial society. Their solution, then, is to move away from the inherited colonial identity and look back to the precolonial past as a source of political inspiration for future national integration. Some Northern Sudanese tend to underestimate the legacy of history that impacted the relationship between the north and the south. Instead of transcending the colonially created racial identities of African and Arab, northern ruling elites tend to emphasize the assimilation of the south in the northern Arab-Islamic identity. For instance, Abdel Wahab El-Affendi stated:

> [the] first leader of the Sudanese Muslim Brotherhood (Ikhwan), Ali Talb allah, was influenced by the romantic vision which coloured the view of early nationalist toward the South . . . [H]e campaigned vigorously for North–South unity in the run-up to the 1942 Juba Conference, and even married a Southern woman to emphasize his commitment to unity.[5]

El-Affendi also refers to the persistence of the colonial mentality among the Southern Sudanese nationalists. He argues that Southerner's self-perception was purely negative; they saw themselves simply as non-northerners. The first Southern Sudanese nationalist movement, he argues, "found no appellation more suitable to adopt than the Sudanese African Closed Districts National Union."[6] This is partly true, but what El-Affendi has failed to see is the legacy of both enslavement and colonialism in framing the way in which southern nationalists resisted the northern domination in the postcolonial state. As a result, these leaders of the early southern nationalist movement failed to go beyond the racialized view of the country and the colonially created ethnic and regional consciousness. These competing discourses on history and identity raise the following question: How do we make sense of these competing claims of nationalisms in the context of the Sudan for instance?

In the Sudan, the competing claims of nationalisms are intricately linked to the process of state formation. In the 1930s, while the British colonial government was gradually institutionalizing an African identity in the South through the policy of indirect rule, a new politics of Arab nationalism emerged in the north. Since the 1930s, the emergent northern-based elites have supported a specific vision of history and identity based on Arabism and Islamism.[7] The struggle over history and identity also raised the question of which kind of social groups inside Sudan were entitled to speak on behalf of the Sudanese people. Instead of transcending them, northern elites, however, reproduced the colonially institutionalized racialized identities. The northern-based nationalist movement of the 1930s created for itself a genealogy that stretched far into the Islamic Arab past. It suggested a primordial and essential identity shared by all those who lived in the north regardless of their particular historical experiences. In response to the British idea of separation between Egypt and the Sudan, a group of junior government officials led by Ali Abd al-latif, a Muslim Dinka military officer, formed the League of Sudan Union in 1922.[8] The League of Sudan Union, however, was splintered in the latter half of 1923 because of a disagreement over the nature of Sudanese identity. Different members of the union had competing visions and interpretations of history and identity.

During this period, the question of race and descent became very significant in determining the course of Sudanese nationalism. Being an Arab became a criterion for citizenship and leadership in Sudanese nationalism. As a Dinka Muslim, Ali Abd al-latif was thought to speak for no one by northern religious leaders such as Abd al-Rahman al-Mahdi. Consequently, the perception of the Sudan as an Arab and Islamic nation became a contested issue among nationalist groups. Thus, Abd al-latif believed that Arab tribal and Islamic religious leaders in the north could represent neither the regions like the south and the Nuba Mountains nor the people from these regions who were living in Northern Sudan. By 1930, however, the vision of the Sudan as an Arab nation had become the dominant principle in discourse among northern elites. The *Hadarat al Sudan*, the Sudan's first independent Arabic newspaper founded in 1920, asked, "what lowly nation is this that is now being led by people of the ilk of Abd al-latif? From what ancestry did this man descend to merit such fame? And of what tribe does he belong?"[9]

Both northern and southern nationalists did not confront legacies of slavery and colonialism during the decolonization process. Instead, racial identities informed by the histories of enslavement and indirect rule were taken for granted and used as mobilizing factors for resistance. In other words, legacies of the precolonial and the colonial periods came to structure the manner in which northern and southern nationalists articulated their competing political visions about the national identity of the postcolonial state. After the political independence of the Sudan in 1956, the dominant ruling elites sought political legitimacy through the discourse of nation-building. This discourse was informed by the exclusive nationalist vision of history and identity. Accordingly, the postcolonial state became closely associated with Islam and Arabism.[10]

Postcolonial State and Political Violence in the Southern Sudan

At the time of independence, the structure of the Sudanese state, its organic law, its institutions, and the basic divisions of power remained as before. Successive military and civilian regimes have exercised power based on the notion that only a Muslim state can

legitimately rule over a Muslim majority. In the process of enforcing this exclusive vision of nation and state, acts of terror and brutal
violence have become the driving force for the state-sponsored
project of nation-building in the Sudan. The exclusive interpretations of history and identity were translated into state policies
during the 1956 debate on the constitution. For instance, the
head of the Sharia Division of the judiciary argued that "the
Sudan constitution must reflect the Islamic and Arab tradition of
the Sudan."[11] Thus, the Sudan came to be seen as an Arab Islamic
state with a civilizing mission of Arabization and Islamization.

Indeed, the transition toward independence had institutionalized the political hegemony of the north and marginalized the
south. Given legacies of slavery and colonialism, civil war in the
Sudan was predictable. During the transition to political independence, Southern Sudanese nationalists argued that the unity with
the north could be accepted on the ground that the system would
be federal, and based on the premise of "an Afro-Arab state with
two distinct personalities, cultures, and temperaments, Negroid
and Arab."[12] Despite Southern Sudanese efforts demanding federalism to prevent northern occupation, the government decided to
send its troops to the south in August 1955. About 300 Southerners
were executed and about 2,000 were transported to northern pris-
ons for hard labor without fair trail.[13] The revolt of 1955 marked
the first phase of the Sudan's civil war, which lasted 17 years.

The initial demand of the southern nationalists was regional
political recognition rather than separation. In fact, this position
did not reject the existence of Arab and African as racial categories;
instead, it demanded the establishment of a political system based
on regionalism that could enable both "races" to coexist in a federal state. This regional option was stated in Ezboni Mondiri's
draft of the Federal Party's Platform during the election campaign
for the first Constituent Assembly in 1958. In his draft, Mondiri
called for official recognition of Christianity and English on a par

with Islam and Arabic. He further demanded separate adminis-trative, educational, and developmental programs for the South.[14] These political demands were developed further by the Anya Nya rebellion, which started on November 30, 1963. The Anya Nya was the military wing of the Sudan African National Union (SANU), founded in 1961 by William Deng.[15]

In 1958, after only two years of independence, Abboud's military coup put an end to what was perceived as a weak civilian government. Indeed, the formation of a military regime marked a new era of violence and discrimination directed toward the peo-ples of Southern Sudan.[16] The military regime perceived political independence as a tool for maintaining the Sudan's territorial "integrity" and removing an artificial barrier to the march of Islam and Arab civilization in the Southern Sudan. Thus, the strategy of the military regime of inventing the soul of "national integration" was based on the assimilation of southerners to Northern Sudanese cultural patterns. As a result, the northern politicians perceived the rise of the southern nationalist movement in the 1960s and its military resistance as part of an external plot against the integrity of the country. Indeed, the integrity of the country meant the imposition of a racialized state in a country with multiple histories and identities.

In response to this discourse, Ismail el-Azhari, the first prime minister, asserted Arab-Islamic identity in his speech to the Roundtable Conference in 1965. He argued:

We are proud of our Arab origin, of our Arabism and of being Moslems. The Arabs came to this continent, as pioneers, to dis-seminate a genuine culture, and promote sound principles which have shed enlightenment and civilization throughout Africa at a time when Europe was plunged into the abyss of darkness, igno-rance and doctrinal and scholarly backwardness. It is our ances-tors who held the torch high and led the caravan of liberation and advancement; and it is they who provided a superior melting-pot for Greek, Persian and Indian culture, giving them the chance to react with all that was noble in Arab culture, and handing them back to the rest of the world as a guide to those who wished to extend the frontiers of learning.[17]

The acts of violence and terror against mostly innocent civilians in Southern Sudan intensified during the civilian government of Mohammed Ahmed Mahgoub (1966–1968), who claimed that the "only language southerners understand is force."[18] During his regime, villages were burned and thousands of people fled to neighboring countries. One of the most ruthless massacres committed by the government's forces occurred at Juba on July 8–9, 1965, when an estimated 1,400 people were killed. The total number of Southerners killed between 1963 and 1966 by the government's forces was estimated at more than 500,000. The rise of violence against Southern Sudanese civilians strengthened the call for a session within the SANU in the mid-1960s.

The Addis Ababa Agreement of March 27, 1972, which temporarily stopped the civil war, was based on the concept of the regionalism of the 1950s, recognizing the south as a distinct cultural and historical identity.[19] Although the agreement had recognized the specificity of Southern Sudanese historical experiences, it reproduced the colonial perception about the south as racially, culturally, and fundamentally different from the north; hence, it deserved separate political and administrative arrangements. This was a postcolonial version of the Southern Sudan's 'policy, which was implemented by the British in 1930. The agreement considered the civil war as an administrative problem rather than a national problem linked to the nature of the postcolonial state. The Addis Ababa agreement gave the South regional autonomy within the framework of a united Sudan. However, the new self-government was based on homogenizing the north as Arab and the south as African, which did not reflect the real situation in the country.[20]

In the course of the following decade, however, the autonomy of the southern region was curtailed. There was an attempt by the Nimeri's regime of 1969–1984 to redraw the boundaries to include the oil-bearing areas in the North. The acts of violence and racial discrimination toward people of the South, however, increased dramatically when the Nimeri' regime unilaterally dissolved the southern regional government and institutionalized *Sharia* law in 1983. As a result, a revolt ensued in the South with the SPLA/M gradually emerging as the principal opposition to the Khartoum government. The SPLA/M political discourse claimed that it was not a separatist movement, but one that sought to unite the whole country along political lines that transcended regional, ethnic, and racial interests.[21] The SPLA/M's manifesto stated that it had "a nation-wide goal and a definite ideological objective of socioeconomic and political development for the whole Sudan."[22]

By 1983, state-sponsored violence against the south was given increasingly religious justification. Since then, civilian and military leaders in the north often have used the language of *jihad* (holy war) in speeches to their followers to justify acts of terror, violence, and discrimination. For instance, the period of Sadiq El Mahdi (1986–1989) witnessed the increased use of Arab militia (*Murahalin*) against people of the Southern Sudan.[23] With the support of the state, these forces attacked mainly civilians and looted their cattle. Sadly, as a result of Sadiq's militia policy, southern civilians were massacred in Al-Da'ein in south Darfur on March 27–28, 1987. Local militias killed more than 1,000 Dinka civilians. Consequently, many Southern Sudanese children were taken and sold into slavery.[24]

A military coup in June 1989 in Khartoum brought to power a fundamentalist regime of the National Islamic Front (NIF) and its leader Omer El-Bashir, who imposed Arabization and Islamization on the entire country through the policy of *jihad*. The new political development forced the SPLA/M in the 1990s to demand "the establishment of two confederal, and sovereign states in the Sudan."[25] John Garang, the chairman of the SPLA/M, has argued that such an arrangement "would solve the sticking point of sharia laws which the . . . NIF government was not willing to relinquish."[26] Since 1989, the government of the National Islamic Front has begun to institutionalize the social, economic, and political foundation of the Islamic state in the Sudan through the policy of forced Arabization and Islamization. The Islamic government has pursued a *jihad* against the south and the civil war has escalated. The government has also systematically encouraged slavery and the revival of slave trading. Militias organized by the government have sold into slavery hundreds of thousands of civilians, mostly women and children, from the Southern Sudan and the Nuba Mountains. The government's forces also routinely steal women and children, and many of the women are subjected to rape or are kept as concubines, while others are shipped north where they perform forced labor on farms or are exported to other Arab countries. Moreover, discrimination in the north by the government against several million displaced southerners has been common as well. By the end of the twentieth century, the total number of people who have died in the Southern Sudan as a result of the postcolonial state's acts of violence and discrimination is more than 2 million. At least one in every five southerners has died.[27]

Thus, the current spread of political violence in the Sudan can be traced to two historical factors—the nature of the postcolonial state, and the form of resistance that was led by nationalist groups to challenge the state. In the Sudan, the state embodies two historical characteristics—violence and racism. When violence is deeply embedded in the foundational structure of the state, the survival of the state, as a racialized institution, largely depends on the use of violence as a mechanism for legitimacy and oppression. However, the failure of those who were subjected to violence and racism to move away from the politics of ethnic and racial nationalism has also prevented the institutionalization of citizenship in the Sudan.

In the Sudan, the northern-based nationalist movement of the 1930s articulated their vision of the postcolonial state in an exclusivist discourse, which perceived the identity of the state and the nation as Arab-Islamic. Consequently, many ethnic groups, the Southern Sudanese in particular, who refused to embrace the Arab-Islamic identity and attempted to maintain their traditions and cultures felt excluded from the postcolonial state. Several strategies were/are used by the state to impose its official exclusive version of identity—the policy of forced Islamization and Arabization, ethnic genocide and slavery, and the slave trade, for example.

Since British colonialism was seen as the root cause of civil war in the Sudan, many northern intellectuals never bothered addressing and confronting the racist practices in their country. For instance, Mohamed Ahmed Mahgoub, a former prime minister, claims that under the British and the missionaries,

> [T]he Southern Sudan had been out of bounds to northern Sudanese, even for ordinary visits, except by special permission. The Northern Sudanese, especially the enlightened class, were aware of British efforts in the thirties to isolate the South, and help the missionaries in the area. Worst of all the missionaries there were the Roman Catholics, who tried to open up old wounds by telling the Southerners that the "Northern Arabs" were the children and grandchildren of the slave-dealers of yore who had sold their father and grandfathers into slavery.[28]

For many Northern Sudanese intellectuals who supported the vision of an Arab-Islamic state, the desirable solution to what they perceived as "ethnic" and "regional" conflict was the gradual disappearance of Africans by way of their assimilation into the mainstream

Arab-Islamic society. Underlying this solution was a racist premise regarding cultural and racial superiority and predominance of Arab descent, propositions leading to the expectation of an eventual elimination of non-Arab groups. In reaction to this Arab nationalism, Africanism has been embraced in the Southern Sudan and more recently in the western region of Darfur as an alternative.

Indeed, there is a relationship between the nature and meaning of nationalism and the spread of political violence in the African continent. The political history of the Sudan has also demonstrated the link between the process of state formation and political identities. The nature of the centralized state that emerged in the nineteenth century in the Sudan not only produced competing political identities but also determined the nature and the content of nationalism. The precolonial legacy of slavery and the colonial policy of indirect rule have contributed to the production of "Arabism" and "Africanism" as competing political identities that are closely linked to the state. These political and racial identities are a product of the history of slavery and the politics of colonialism. Both historical circumstances have also conditioned the way in which nationalism evolved. Instead of mobilizing different groups around the notion of citizenship and equal rights, nationalists instead advocated an exclusive vision of a nation that divides its people into two categories—citizens and subjects.

CHAPTER 4

EXILE, IDENTITY, AND
POLITICAL REFORM

Our history with the Arab since the self-rule in 1953 should remind you clearly that the enemy means no peace. Enemy reinforcements and bombings are going on, as they talk peace. The history of the struggle to be free from the Arabs must be taught to the children, while in exile. We who are inside are already living this history from day to day through constant enemy attacks. These are grave times and we should refrain from considering enemy pretences and instead focus on hard work in order to achieve our destiny of total freedom.[1]

It is, of course true that the African identity is still in the making. There isn't a final identity that is African. But, at the same time, there is an identity coming into existence. And it has a certain context and a certain meaning.[2]

The civil war in the Southern Sudan has led to the massive displacement of about 5.5 million Sudanese. About 2.1 million of these people live in shantytowns within the country, especially around Khartoum, the capital city. There are also about 2 million who are displaced within the South, both in the areas held by the SPLA and the government garrison towns. The rest took refuge in neighboring countries mainly Uganda, Kenya, Democratic Republic of Congo, Central African Republic, and Egypt.

Since the late 1980s, Egypt has witnessed an increasing number of refugees from both the North and the South Sudan, peoples who were forced to leave their country because of the

Islamic regime's policy of oppression, the civil war, and the economic difficulties that resulted from it. Despite this growing number of Sudanese refugees in Egypt, there are no reliable statistics on the number of Sudanese in Egypt.[3] In Egypt, Cairo plays an important role for the Sudanese diaspora, particularly because southern and northern opposition political groups already have established a strong base in the city.

Until July 4, 1995, the Egyptian government did not treat Sudanese citizens as refugees in Egypt, instead calling them "citizens in their second home." On July 4, 1995, following accusations that the Sudanese government was behind the June 29, 1995 assassination attempt on President Hosni Mubarak, the Egyptian government issued a presidential decree requiring all Sudanese entering Egypt to apply for a visa.[4] Problems between Sudan's Islamic regime and the Egyptian government accelerated when Egypt accused Sudan of training "fundamentalist terrorists" and sending them across the border. Sudan responded by expelling all Egyptian teachers, and nationalizing Egyptian institutions, such as the Khartoum branch of Cairo University, and cutting off all stipends to Sudanese university students in Egypt.

The majority of Southern Sudanese refugees came to Egypt after the military coup of 1989, which was led by the NIF. Most refugees had lived in Khartoum as displaced persons before leaving for Egypt. A letter from a Southern Sudanese group in Egypt described their journey from Southern Sudan to Egypt as follows:

> To arrive in Egypt, the southern Sudanese first would invariably begin the journey into exile by fleeing out of his home in the south to the presumed "safer" Northern part of Sudan. But, to his/her horror and disbelief, even there in the so-called "safer" area, he/she is subjected to persistent harassment, persecution and denial of his inalienable rights by the same authorities that victimized him in the South. So, inevitably, the Southern Sudanese finally flees to Egypt.[5]

They came to Cairo either by train or air. They lived either in extended households, many female-headed, or as students sharing cheap flats. They lived in apartments in lower socioeconomic areas of the city, in the same neighborhoods as poor and uneducated Egyptians. A former professor from Juba University, living in one of these neighborhoods for three years, expressed his frustration thus:

> I couldn't imagine myself five or six years ago that I would be one day living in this neighborhood. You can hardly find one person who can make sense of the world here. Yes, we are poor like them now, but at least we can read, write, and understand our situation in exile. It's a painful thing for me to experience in my life. Sometimes I feel it is better for me to go home and live among my displaced people than go through this suffering.[6]

Since 1983, many Southern Sudanese have been mentally and physically abused by the government policies toward the south. Some of them spoke of how northern security forces treated them in South Sudan. One recounted, "people often were taken by the security or army in the middle of the night and never seen again." This experience of pain and the ways in which it is interpreted contributes to their sense of themselves as Southern Sudanese. One of my respondents recounted:

> I came to Egypt in 1993, when I was in Juba—southern Sudan; I worked as an army officer. In Juba I saw many people had been taken by the security forces, some were beaten, tortured and killed. The security forces of the government see southern Sudanese either as SPLA/M agents or foreign agents. Some of my friends were accused by the government and put to death. When the situation became worse, I decided to come to Egypt.[7]

The pain was not only physical but also psychological. Southern Sudanese in Egypt exist in a state of insecurity as they struggled to re-create their identity. In this environment of insecurity they are constantly under surveillance by the host country's authorities.

The main source of income for many displaced Southern Sudanese men is activities in nonformal sectors of the Egyptian economy. These activities include low paying jobs at construction sites and small-scale jobs at home, such as basket making.

> The only casual employees paid higher wages, slightly more than L.E. 10 daily (about $2.5), are those working underground in Metro and Sewage construction sites . . . Health wise this job is very dangerous . . . Fatalities have been witnessed in the past among the displaced Sudanese.[8]

However, in spite of their economic hardships, Egypt, especially Cairo, became a center for refugee communities and organizations. Two reasons may explain the development of Southern Sudanese communities in Egypt. First, cut off from their roots, their land, and their past, refugees felt an urgent need to reconstitute their broken lives. Second, Egypt's relative freedom of expression and association provided an opportunity to freely exchange feelings and ideas about the war and exile, and thus helped to begin restructuring their shattered world.

Exile, Identity, and Place

Scholars in anthropology and cultural studies have explored the relationship between movement, exile, and identity. Iain Chambers has argued that "our sense of being, of identity and language, is experienced and extrapolated from movement: the 'I' does not pre-exist this movement and then go out into the world, the 'I' is constantly being formed and reformed in such movement in the world."[9] Madan Sarap has pointed out that when migrants cross a boundary, or a new frontier, and are faced with a hostile reception, they draw in on themselves and reinforce their own culture, their collective identity.[10] Thus, one question I wish to explore in this chapter is whether Southern Sudanese in exile become more imbued with new cultural and political identities as opposed to what were colonially created ethnic identities. Another question is to what extent have Southern Sudanese turned the state of exile and displacement into a way of resistance? Resistance, as Edward Said put it, "is an alternative way of conceiving human history,"[11] thus opening the way for rewriting history and imagining the future of returning to the homeland.

Refugees, however, do not discover their identities in exile. Instead they redefine them by acts of self-representation that are often political. Edward Said argues thus:

> The construction of identity is bound up finally with the disposition of power and powerlessness in each society, and what makes all the fluid and extraordinarily rich actualities of identity difficult to accept is that most people resist the underlying notion that human identity is not only not natural and stable but constructed and occasionally even invented outright.[12]

Southern Sudanese refugees in Egypt share a number of commonalties: their origins and continuing attachment to the places of Southern Sudan,[13] the collective experience of displacement, and a concept and practice of national resistance. Host country settings have acted to add another dimension to Southern Sudanese identity.[14] Exile and the specificity of host population–refugee interactions have become salient factors in Southern Sudanese identity, incorporating feelings of otherness, discrimination, and marginalization. Many refugees felt that the host population had treated them as a racial inferior, a political alien, and a cultural outsider. A Southern Sudanese mother of three described her feeling in Egypt:

> I was born in Juba where I lived among my people. Our life in Juba was wonderful. Everybody knew everybody; even during the

war we had not experienced difficulties like what we are facing in Egypt. Life is difficult here, and we don't feel being respected as human beings. Our daily life here is causing us a lot of pains and miseries.[15]

Yet, places of exile are also sites of resistance to displacement and the construction of desired identities away from the exclusionary or hegemonic state. Therefore, in the context of exile, Southern Sudanese realized the fact that individuals in any society carry the potential for multiple forms of identities whether these are gender, age, class, race, regional origin, kinship, religion, sexuality, and so on.[16] A young Southern Sudanese student living in Cairo said,

I have learnt many things in Egypt. In the South, I used to see myself as a Southerner who belongs to the Dinka tribe. But here in Egypt, I am not only a Southerner and a Dinka person, but also a refugee, black, African and student living in one of the poorest areas in Egypt.[17]

Redefining a "Southern Sudanese" in Egypt

In chapter 2, I charted out how the people of South Sudan were transformed from flexible cultural communities to African or southerners through the legacies of enslavement and colonialism. In Egypt, however, Southern Sudanese redefined their identities, first through undergoing the hardship of exile and achieving moral worthiness and second, through liberating their homeland and resisting assimilation.

As Egypt began to find itself an unwelcome host to a large number of refugees from Sudan, Southern Sudanese experienced Egyptian hostility. Historically, Egypt has not considered the struggle of the South Sudan sympathetically, regarding the establishment of an independent state in the South Sudan a threat to the "unity of the Nile Valley."[18] Therefore, Egyptian foreign policy rejects Southern Sudanese claims for self-determination and favors a united Sudan. Egypt, like other Arab countries, perceives Southern Sudan as an obstacle toward the expansion of Arab and Islamic civilization to eastern and southern Africa.

In addition to being unwelcome and politically unfavored by the Egyptian people and government, Southern Sudanese also faced the problem of being non-Arabs and non-Muslims living in an Arab-Islamic society. A former police officer described his experience with his Egyptian landlord in the following way:

> My landlord is an old woman; she has five grandsons. She is a very devoted Muslim. Although she rented her apartment to so many Sudanese, she does not consider me Sudanese because I am not a Muslim. She thinks Sudanese people are all Muslims. She speaks Egyptian Arabic, and I do speak Arabic like many Northern Sudanese. Any time we chat together, she asked me to convert to Islam. I told her several times that I am a Christian. One day she said that if I am a Sudanese, I should be a Muslim.[19]

Refugees found their rights to work, travel, and engage in political activities constrained by the Egyptian government. Work permits, necessary to be legally employed, were impossible to obtain, while political activities and organizations had to conform to Egyptian government policies. One of my respondents recounted how the Egyptian government treated them differently from the Northern Sudanese who were also refugees in Egypt.

> Northern politicians can practice politics freely and organize meetings without restrictions. For us—Southern Sudanese— we don't have this freedom. We can't organize political meetings easily except in church buildings. The Egyptian security forces deported many Southern Sudanese because of their political affiliations.[20]

One of my respondents said, "we, Dinka, Nuer, Kuku, Bari, and others, we all Southern Sudanese. We suffered from those

Northerners. Today we live in Cairo because of them, what we need is just freedom for our people."[21] Another respondent gave a historical reason for redefining himself as a Southern Sudanese rather than using his ethnic group name: "I am a Southern Sudanese because [of] the name Nuer. . . . was what the British named us because we were considered savage and warlike."[22] Thus, it is in exile that Southern Sudanese have experienced themselves being collectively identified as Southerners. Egyptians do not see Southern Sudanese in terms of different ethnic groups.

In Egypt, like many other Arab countries, color plays a very significant role in identifying and determining a person's status. Being "black" in the Egyptian society has negative consequences.[23] One young Southern Sudanese argued

> Egyptians call us *Samara* (black). When we walk in the street, they call us names, even their children do that, and they some-times attack us physically. They don't even differentiate between us. They only know one thing; we are all *Samara* and inferior to them. When we go to the police to report an abuse, the police officer doesn't take us seriously, and sometimes even they chase us away.[24]

Being Southern Sudanese in Egypt means having experienced displacement and suffering; it means being a struggler and a sur-vivor. A respondent told me that "there is not a Southerner in Egypt who had lived through the current Islamic regime who did not lose a relative or a friend to civil war, starvation, disease, or exe-cution." Southern Sudanese processes of collectivity focus on the reestablishment of ties with family and friends, practicising indige-nous customs, and creating a social environment in which the reconstituted identities can be expressed in language, social rela-tions, food, music, and ritual. These widespread social practices among the refugees have reinforced the emotions, memories, and legitimacy of their political and cultural struggles.

Southern Sudanese Communities and Organizations in Egypt

Of course, the community as a formation of cultural practices, a process of associational life, and as a moral entity is historically and socially constructed. The traditional values and institutions of Southern Sudan are largely authoritarian, patriarchal, and ethnic. In the context of exile, however, the process of community formation has been given a new meaning. Although Southern Sudanese refugees in Egypt were subjected to numerous legal disabilities and severe economic difficulties, they nevertheless formed many new organisations with cultural and political goals and for mutual aid and economic self-help. The purpose of forming these organizations was to reconstruct and preserve the achievement of the Southern Sudanese, and to restructure the basis for its continuing development. By the time I conducted my research, there were about 34 informal groups established by the Southern Sudanese refugees in Egypt. Most of these were based on ethnic, regional, cultural, or gender identification. Some were formed for income-generating and humanitarian purposes.

The ethnic-based organizations played a significant role in teaching the various Southern Sudanese indigenous languages to a younger generation.[25] Some groups established language-teaching classes at the Sacred Heart Church in 1992. The cultural associations also promoted the cultural rituals and practices of the Southern Sudan, challenging the idea that Southern Sudanese had no culture and history. Southern Sudanese used various strategies to reconstruct and preserve their culture and heritage. For instance, the representative of the African Cultural Society in Cairo stated that one of its objectives was "to promote African woman to protect her rights and encourage her to fully participate in the society."[26] Other groups such as, the Daniel Comboni Show Jazz Band,[27] the Akwa Group, and the Azande Dancing

Group celebrated the Southern Sudanese musical and dance heritage. Their songs reflect the Southern Sudanese experiences of displacement whether in the Sudan or in exile.

Church, Christianity, and the "Southern Sudanese" Identity

The pressure from political Islam in the North has contributed to the expansion of Christianity in the South.[28] The Southern Sudanese see Christianity as a strong political, social, and cultural movement against the north. The assertion of political Islam in the north, and the identification of the ruling Islamic regime with the Arab-Islamic worldview, invited the Southern Sudanese to present their ideology of resistance in a similar way.

Displacement also influenced people's spiritual beliefs. The church in Egypt has played a major role in helping the Southern Sudanese refugees. Catholic and Anglican Churches, such as the Sacred Heart Church, All Saints Cathedral, Saint Andrew's, and many others, provided for some of the displaced people's needs. For instance, the Sacred Heart Church in El Abasiya, together with some active refugees, was able to initiate projects and programs on the church premises in which the refugee community could participate freely, including the Christian Training Center and the Saint Luwanga Education Center.[29] These programs created some educational and job opportunities for the Southern Sudanese refugees. Socially and spiritually, the church also offered the Southern refugees prayer support, Sunday mass, and Bible study. Most importantly, the church provided a space for the refugees to carry out activities, such as Christmas pageants and weddings ceremonies, without interference from the host population. The church provided the Southern Sudanese a sanctuary from the verbal and physical abuse that they routinely faced in the streets.

Before the war, Christianity in South Sudan was associated more with the educated living in towns and largely with the formally employed than with people living in the countryside. However, the civil war of 1983 destroyed this urban life. The administrative and economic functions, which sustained the towns, collapsed. The politicization of Islam by the government in Khartoum made religion a political issue in the Sudan. Consequently, many Southerners have come to see churches as their political allies in struggle against injustice and oppression. One of the most observed social developments among the refugees was a growing Christianization. This trend has increased the numbers of baptized Southern Sudanese in Egypt. Many people explained the reason for their baptism in terms of resisting Islam and Arab domination. One said, "the war is political, but it is a religious conflict also; Christians are dying every day in the Sudan. They want us to become Muslims, but we are Christians."[30]

Unlike Islam in Northern Sudan, religion in Southern Sudan is a personal matter rather than a state affair. In Francis Deng's view:

> Nilotic beliefs and practices are structured along autonomous territorial and descent-oriented units. This provides for autonomous and personal linkages with god through the ancestral spirits, thereby allowing for a measure of religious pluralism and freedom.[31]

In the past, Southern Sudanese saw the Christian mission as a source of literacy and modern skills rather than a provider of spiritual order. In the context of civil war and exile, however, the church is a provider and a protector.[32] Consequently, Christianity among Southern Sudanese is becoming an essential component of their political identity.

Political Identity among
the Southern Sudanese in Exile

Displacement changes people in profound ways. It changes their political perceptions of themselves, other people, and the world. Refugees experience loss, cultural change, and regeneration. The displacement and exile of Southern Sudanese caused by war produced homelessness, diversity, and new identities. Being a refugee also allowed Southern Sudanese to see differences and to see others differently. Southern Sudanese in Egypt realized that there were some groups in the north that also suffered and were brutalized by the Islamic regime. In addition to Southern Sudanese, many Sudanese ethnic groups such as Fur, Beja, and people from the Nuba Mountains have fled to Egypt since 1989. Before coming to Egypt, many Southern Sudanese used to identify these groups as "Northern Sudanese." However, the experience of being a refugee has changed this colonial political perception. Clearly, being a Muslim without being an Arab in the Sudan is not credential enough to be accepted as a member of the "noble Islamic-Arab nation." A Southern Sudanese activist said,

> When I was in the south, I used to divide Sudan into two hostile regions: the North and the South. People who live in the north I considered them all as Arabs and enemies. Today, things have changed, when I came to Egypt, I found many people from the north, (Fur, Nuba, Beja) are also running from the Islamic government. Like us, the government attacked them because they are different. I don't consider them now Arabs anymore.[33]

This new political identity, however, is articulated through an expression of culture distinct from that of Egyptians, and a historical and emotive experience that sharply distinguished them from other Sudanese groups who are living in Egypt:

> For the first time in the history of the Sudan, the Southerners are sharing the same fate of a refugee with the Northern Sudanese,

some of whom were themselves perpetrators in the Sudan tragedy. However, despite the shared commonalties of the current predicament, this new phenomenon does not augur well with the Southern Sudanese. First, in contrast to the Southerners, the people of the North Sudan can easily adapt into the culture and, second, many of them have established economic and family roots in the host country.[34]

As the national liberation movement developed, and Southern Sudanese saw themselves as betrayed politically by the Organization of African Unity and the Arab League and subjected to attacks by Egyptian police and security forces, the form of their cultural and political identities increasingly took on a specifically "Southern Sudanese" orientation.[35] A Southern Sudanese argued:

> Our problem with the north is that Arab people when they came to the Sudan, did not respect the indigenous people. They came to the south Sudan to obtain our people as slaves. They also deceived the British with the help of the Egyptians, to control political power after independence. Today they are trying to destroy our culture and heritage. They want us to be Arabs and Muslims, and they forget that we are southern Sudanese first and African second.[36]

Conceding that they are Africans and as such share general historical and cultural orientations with other peoples of the region, nevertheless Southern Sudanese distinguish themselves from other Africans by reference to certain moral qualities. A woman said to me, "we are Africans, but not like Nigerians," whom she considered morally "corrupt," and "dishonest."[37] Southern Sudanese see themselves as honest and morally strong unlike Northern Sudanese Arabs, whom they consider to be dishonest and possessed of a *Jallaba*'s (Northern Sudanese merchant) mentality. One says, "we can not live with *Mondocrats* (northerners), they are untrusted people."

In exile, the bases of community have not been fixed. The meaning of the space within which the Southern Sudanese community in Egypt was constructed is in flux as well. While one can speak of Southern community in Egypt, one must be careful not to over-generalize and to keep in the forefront the multilayered nature of both community and identity. First, southern refugees came to Egypt from a variety of ethnic groups and regions in South Sudan. A common point of reference for refugees was the past and places of origin in, and a sense of belonging to, the physical and social space of Southern Sudan. The past is not distant from the present, and gives meaning to one's historical sense of self. Those who came to Egypt formed a community of refugees who shared an experience of being refugees in an Arab-Islamic society.

Though a process of cultural and political reconstruction has begun to unfold, the commonality of struggle informed new categories of meaning. The defining quality of the Southern Sudanese culture of resistance is militancy, whose concrete expression is the SPLA/SPLM in all its myriad forms and armed struggles. Since 1994, the SPLA/M has managed to gain the support of an overwhelming majority of Southern Sudanese inside and outside the Sudan.[38] But this support has not been transformed by the SPLA/M into a unified political identity that could cut through the ethnic and racial sentiments. During the earlier years of the movement, the majority of people from the Equatoria region did not support the SPLA/M. Many Equatorians perceived the formation of the SPLA/M as an attempt to restore the Dinka hegemony in the south. Policies of human rights abuses and ethnic nepotism have also contributed to further division and interethnic wars in the South.[39]

Although there is recognition of the existence of multiple ethnic identities among Southern Sudanese, there is also a growing awareness of the commonality of cultural and racial violence against them. It is logical for Southern Sudanese to respond to repression and exploitation by emphasizing the bounded nature of their common historical experiences and their cultural distinctiveness—a sense of separateness, a sense and meaning of the national and cultural self as quite distinct from that of colonial discourse. Despite its weakness, this new identity is intermingled with new forms of political and military organization and categories of meaning to respond to hegemonic racialized structures of the postcolonial state.

Southern Sudanese refugees are learning from their experiences in the Sudan and Egypt to be united as southerners. As one informant said, "we are all here in Egypt for one reason; because we are Southern Sudanese."[40] The Southern Sudanese did not simply discover this consciousness in Egypt; it has been created collectively through long historical struggles. The experience of Southern Sudanese in Egypt has had a particularly serious impact on Southern Sudanese society. Cairo has become a kind of melting pot for Southern Sudanese ethnic groups, and as a leveler of differences and conflicts, which have been present before displacement and exile.

After the Addis Ababa Agreement of 1973, for instance, regionalism had become a threat to southern unity. What changed in Egypt was the scant reference to region among Southern Sudanese refugees. During my research, I learned that Southern Sudanese often regarded regionalism as a creation of the northern-dominated governments, and it was perceived as a problem of the past. A southern politician explained it in this way:

> In the past, our people did not know the threat of factionalism. Our enemy in the north encouraged this regionalism in the south in order to prevent our unity. Today we learn that it is easy to get killed if you are divided into groups, but you will not get killed if you are united.[41]

Southern Sudanese and the Future of the Sudan

When the SPLA/M was formed in 1983, its declared objective was the formation of a new, united Sudan. That is, a new Sudan to which all Sudanese could pledge allegiance irrespective of race, religion, class, or other identities. The movement rejected the old Sudan on the basis that it is exclusively Islamic and Arab. The SPLA/M notion of a "New Sudan" is a critique of Islam as the state religion and the basis of the constitution and public laws of the country; Arabic as the official and national language of the state; and Arabism and Islam as defining factors in national identity. The idea of a new united Sudan dominated the movement's discourse until 1991 when the SPLA/M was split into two groups. The SPLA/M by its nature is not a homogeneous body; it represents different social, cultural, regional, and political groups, with different historical and political backgrounds. After the split of 1991, the SPLA/M introduced the right of self-determination for South Sudan in its political agenda. However, the SPLA/M has reconfigured the border of Southern Sudan to include other marginalized groups.[42]

In June 1995, the SPLA/M and northern opposition groups signed the Asmara Declaration.[43] This declaration laid the foundation for political and military cooperation between the opposition forces from both the north and the south under the National Democratic Alliance (NDA). According to the declaration, confederal and federal arrangements will be put in place in all of Sudan to be followed by a referendum on self-determination in Southern Sudan, Abyei, the Nuba Mountains, and the Ingessena Hills after a four-year interim period.

Although the Northern political forces accepted that the people of these areas should exercise their right to self-determination, many Southern Sudanese expressed fears and doubt about the commitment of these northern parties. A Southern Sudanese commented,

> It is not a matter of agreement between these forces and the SPLA/M, but it is a question of trust and practice. Our history with those political parties was full of crimes and oppression. I don't think they are genuine in this agreement; they are using the SPLA to fight for them the war against the NIF.[44]

Peter A. Nyaba eloquently frames the dilemma of the National Democratic Alliance and the SPLA/M.

> I look at The National Democratic Alliance not as a bridge to the formation of one secular democratic Sudan, but as a convenient forum for a peaceful dismemberment of the Sudan, and the formation of two separate, independent and sovereign entities, just in the same way the Czech and the Slovak republics were formed from the former Czechoslovakia following the collapse of the Soviet Union. The baseline for the NDA is the overthrow of the NIF regime. The people of the Sudan should not re-enact the experiences that have escalated the conflict between the Arab-dominated North and the South. To do that would be as futile as the war the Serbs fought in Croatia and in Bosnia-Herzegovina. The alliance of the SPLM with these parties should be based on clear objectives acceptable to the people of south Sudan.[45]

For many refugees, the idea of a united Sudan reminds them of the human misery and suffering that they have already been through. The old Sudan, inherited from the British colonialism, does not exist in their daily public discourse of national liberation. A respondent argued that:

> You see what is happening now in Eastern Europe. People are freeing themselves from the domination of one group. We cannot accept oppression; we will fight like our elders who fought against the colonial power. Today not only southern Sudanese should fight but also groups such as Fur, Beja, Nuba, and others.[46]

The major change among Southern Sudanese in Egypt was the tendency to emphasize the question of identity in their conflict with the north. During the first civil war of 1955–1972, Southern Sudanese were more concerned with administrative arrangements such as a regional government or a federal system. By the time I conducted my research they were not concerned with these issues anymore. A former civil servant explained this new tendency.

> During the Addis Ababa agreement we thought we could live together with those of the north, but they deceived us, and even succeeded in dividing us into regions and hostile ethnic groups. Instead of treating us as equal partners, they disrespected us and treated us as inferior to them. Thus, our demand today is not getting jobs or posts in government but to protect our culture, history and identity.[47]

The Southern Sudanese in Egypt obviously are engaged in the process of redefining and reconstructing their cultural and political identities. This collective, dynamic process of reconstruction involves redefining themselves and others, and is a product of a historical process of marginalization and resistance. The colonially invented identity of African in Southern Sudan has been given new meaning and content, which questions the colonial and the postcolonial discourse of "otherness." The brutality of the civil war, and the experience of violence and the renewal of slavery and the slave trade have led them to challenge the imposed stereotypes and representations.

The experience of displacement and the contact with the host population have not only strengthened their unity, but also helped them to imagine their future. Experiencing exile in an Arab country has encouraged Southern Sudanese to think of themselves in different terms from other Arabized groups of the Sudan. However, it would be a mistake to regard the "southern identity" as a single entity. Though the Southern Sudanese identity is broadened and deepened by displacement and exile after 1983, the resultant complexity of Southern Sudanese societies cannot be represented by a single entity. For instance, one aspect of the Southern Sudanese resistance in Egypt is that it raises a debate on social and cultural norms that one day would shape a new Southern Sudan. This development is evident in the emergence, on the one hand, of women's activism, marked by a conscious effort to maintain a focus on gender issues,[48] and on the other, of ethnic and cultural groups that put specific emphasis on indigenous languages as part of a broader social and cultural program.

The circumstances of displacement and refugeeness created new concepts of what African and Arab mean in the exile and Sudanese contexts. However, neither culture nor experience is so complete and coherent as to constitute a singular identity. One can speak of the Southern Sudanese of Egypt, Southern Sudanese of Kenya, Southern Sudanese of Uganda, and so on. Unlike the colonially created identity of Southern Sudan in which African identity was exemplified in various ethnicities and referenced solely to a single place of origin, what emerged during my research was a sense of southern identity that was multi-referenced in terms of places of exile. The experience of Southern Sudanese in Egypt has shown that the political and cultural identities of an oppressed racial group change over time, geographical space, and historical content. Consequently, the conception of racial and ethnic categories is being questioned and transformed. That which is termed African or Southern Sudanese by those in power to describe a particular group's racial/ethnic background in a particular space can have little historical or practical meaning within another social and political context that is also racially stratified, but in a different form. Thus, the generalization and the rigid boundaries of racial and ethnic identities of the past no longer make much sense.

CHAPTER 5

THE CRISIS IN DARFUR AND THE NORTH–SOUTH PEACE PROCESS

Nearly a million people have been displaced from their homes in western Sudan; many have fled into neighboring Chad. They say militias working with the Sudanese government have been attacking villages, ransacking and torching homes, killing and raping civilians. These armed forces are supposedly cracking down on rebel groups, but in fact they are targeting the population.
—Carroll Bogert, *The Houston Chronicle*, May 4, 2004

The recent political violence in the western region of Darfur demonstrates the complexity of the Sudan's tragedy. While the GOS and the SPLA/M are negotiating to end the longest running civil war in the South, a new civil war erupted in the region of Darfur. There are signs that the GOS and the SPLA/M are searching for a comprehensive peace agreement to end the longest running civil war in the south. Supported by the United States of America and other African and Western countries, the peace negotiations between the GOS and the SPLA/M, however, have focused on outstanding north–south conflicts over identity, power and wealth sharing, and the future of the three contested regions of the Nuba Mountains, Blue Nile, and Southern Kordofan. But the north–south conflict is only one of the many regional conflicts that have devastated Sudan. Furthermore, political parties within and outside the NDA have contested the SPLA/M and the Sudan government's monopoly of peace negotiations, labeling them as nondemocratic in their handling of issues pertinent to the future of the whole country.

The Darfur conflict began early in 2003, when two armed movements, Sudan Liberation Army/Movement (SLA/M) and the Justice and Equality Movement (JEM), began a rebellion against government policies in Khartoum that have marginalized the Darfur region. Unlike the SPLA/M, both movements do not demand self-determination. Instead, they seek equitable development, land rights, social and public services, democracy, and regional autonomy. For instance, the SLA/M stated its position on the system of governance as follows:

> The SLM/A shall struggle to achieve a decentralized form of governance based on the right of Sudan's different regions to govern themselves autonomously through a federal or confederal system. At the same time the Central Government must be completely restructured and recast so that it adequately reflects Sudan's rich diversity as represented by the component regions, which are its stakeholders.[1]

In response to the rebellion, the Islamized and Arabized government in Khartoum mobilized and armed a militia group, known as *Janjaweed*,[2] employing scorched-earth, massacre, and starvation as strategies to defeat the rebel groups. The violence in Darfur has led to the killing of more than 50,000 and displacement of over 1 million civilians. The UN has described the situation in Darfur as "the world's worst humanitarian crisis"; the U.S. Congress and the State Department described it as "genocide."[3] As a result, observers of the Sudan's affairs have begun to question the feasibility of the current peace negotiations between the GOS and the SPLA/M. For instance, Susan Rice and Gayle Smith said,

> The [US] administration has worked hard to end Sudan's long running civil conflict. But this effort will have been wasted if we allow the Sudanese government to continue committing crimes

against humanity. Not only will the international community have blood on its hand for failure to halt another genocide, but we will have demonstrated to Khartoum that it can continue to act with impunity against its own people. In that case, any hard-won peace agreement will not be worth the paper it's signed on.[4]

The conflict in Darfur has indeed exemplified the simplicity of the view that often casts the Sudan's conflict in terms of south versus north or African against Arab. The crisis in Darfur has also revealed the inability of the north–south paradigm in explaining the root causes of the conflict. As I argued in chapter 1, for decades scholars and policy makers of the Sudan have struggled to grapple with the question of civil war in the Sudan. However, few have managed to free themselves from the shackles of the colonial discourse, which divide the country into supposedly two distinct racial, cultural, and religious entities.

Very often the recent political violence in Darfur is perceived as a war between Arabs and "black"/African Muslims. Stephen Nolen, for instance, went further to claim that "the Africans are farmers, while Arab tribes are nomadic herders."[5] This view certainly misrepresents the reality of the conflict. The conflict in Darfur is in fact a manifestation of the national crisis that has ravaged the country for decades. The root causes of the conflict have a long history and politics associated with the process of state formation and its impacts on the politics of identity in the Sudan. This national crisis first arose in the South Sudan in 1955, when the first phase of the civil war began.

When the conflict erupted in Darfur in 2003, many in the Western media and commentators on the Sudanese affairs were either caught by surprise or were unable to make sense of the violence. On the one hand, in the minds of those who always assert the religious factor in the Sudan's civil war, the conflict in Darfur is incomprehensible. After all, the people of Darfur are devoted Muslims, and presumably belong to the larger Muslim world.

However, the brutality of the violence that was inflicted on Muslims of Darfur forced Frida Ghitis to ask, "[if] Muslim countries claim to worry so much about the fate of Muslims in other places, why do they do absolutely nothing when the black Muslims of Darfur die at the hand of Arab Muslims?"[6]

On the other hand, in the minds of those who tend often to perceive the conflict in racial terms, African versus Arab, the Darfur crisis is unthinkable because the people of Darfur are known as Arab in the context of the north–south conflict. In both perceptions, history and politics has been removed from the context of the conflict. Sadly, in the mind of the perpetrators and the victims, the conflict in Darfur is also presented as a war between Arab and Black/African Muslims. In both cases, the racial categories Arab and Black/African are taken for granted. The role of the state in creating and enforcing them as political identities has been ignored. Instead, the warring groups in Darfur have used these categories to advance their political goals in the context of competing histories and identities. For the perpetrators or the killers—the government and the armed militias—the term Arab enables them to mobilize their people along a perceived racial line by creating an environment of fear among the Arab groups. One of the militia leaders, Musa Hilal for instance, told new recruits for the *Janjaweed* militia in the town of Kapkabiya: "this area is in danger, and we need volunteers to defend it from the rebels." He also said, "*Zurga* [black] support the rebels. We should defeat the rebels." The leaders of the government backed militia group use songs and poetry to rally their followers against the non-Arab groups.[7]

For the victims—rebel groups and innocent civilians from non-Arab groups—the term African or black makes their case not only acceptable to the Western world, but also enables them to forge a sense of solidarity under a political identity in opposition to Arab identity. A refugee from Darfur argues, "the government wants to kill all African people, Muslim or not Muslim, in order to put Arabs in their places . . . we Africans are good Muslims. We pray all the time. We read Koran all the time. It is they who are bad Muslims."[8] Another refugee stated, "they [*janjaweed*] want to steal things and they want to kill us. They want the black people out because they want to take our land to live on," and he went on to say, "[it's] because they don't want black people—they want Sudan to be for Arab people. They will get the herders to come and take our land." This is in fact not to deny the existence of both terms Arab and African in the local context prior to the recent violence in the region. However, these terms African/ black or "*Zurga*" and Arab are produced through long historical and political processes in which the state has been an active participant.

As I have argued in chapter 2, neither race, nor culture is at the center of the current Sudan's crisis. Instead, it is the racialized postcolonial state that imposed a single vision of nation through the policy of Arabization and Islamization. The social and the cultural history of Darfur has shown that the process of periodical migrations and the cultural practice of intermarriages between various cultural communities has created flexible cultural and social identities that have blurred racial, cultural, and religious boundaries. The labels of Arab and African do not fit the social and economic realities of Darfur. R.S. O'Fahey has argued,

> Darfur comprises three ethnic "zones"; the northern zone includes Arab and non-Arab (mainly Zaghawa and Bideyat) camel nomads. The central zone on both sides of the Jabal Marra mountain range is inhabited largely by non-Arab sedentary farmers such as the Fur, Masalit and others, cultivating millet and speaking their own languages, while in the south there are series of Arabic-speaking cattle nomads—the Baqqara. All are Muslim and no part of Darfur was ever ethnically homogenous. For example, a successful Fur farmer would invest in cattle; once the cattle

reached a certain number, it would be more profitable to cross the ethnic frontier and "become" Baqqara and in a few generations his descendants would have an "authentically" Arab genealogy.[9]

In the past, differences between ethnic groups were not given so much emphasis. There were intermarriages between communities who spoke Arabic as their first language and communities who spoke a traditional African language. Carter Dougherty argues, "[c]enturies of intermarriage has rendered the two groups physically indistinguishable, but al-Bashir's Khartoum regime is Arab dominated."[10] The politization of religion and the racialization of cultural differences predictably led to tension and the spread of violence in the region of Darfur. In the violence that has engulfed the region since early 2003, "race" has become a cruel reality. In fact, the violence that is unfolding in Darfur is the same violence that has happened in Southern Sudan for the last 20 years. Of course, there is one difference between the war in the south and the war in Darfur. It is true that, "[the] ethnic Africans of Darfur, unlike those of the South, are Muslim. And not just Muslim: deeply, devoutly, unshakably Muslim."[11] Although the people of Darfur are Muslims, they have been subjected to discrimination and racism. In Central Sudan, for instance, people often refer to people from Darfur in inferior terms due to their non-Arab origin. As I have indicated in chapter 2, derogatory terms such as *Gharaba* (Westerners) or *Fallata* are frequently used to refer to people of Darfur and western African immigrants. In the context of the Sudan, origin rather than religion determines the identity of the person. For instance, being non-Arab and Muslim does not give the people of Darfur equal status with their fellow Arab Muslims in central Sudan.

Unlike the people of Southern Sudan, many people of Darfur, despite their non-Arab origin, have embraced an Arab identity in the past. Although they share the same history of oppression, marginalization, and injustices, they thought of embracing Arabism as a way to distance themselves from Southern Sudanese who have been stigmatized by the legacy of slavery. Since the eruption of the first civil war in the South in 1955, the national army, under the banner of Islam and Arabism, has relied on people from Darfur in its war against Southern Sudanese. Over 40 percent of the national army comes from the region of Darfur. The strategy of the government is to pit one non-Arab group against another and prevent the unity of the marginalized and subordinated people. This strategy is commonly known in the Sudan's popular culture as *"Aktul al-abid bil abid"*—"kill the slave through the slave."

Neither of the two wars in the south, nor the current conflict in Darfur, are aberrations. Instead, these wars should be viewed as the inevitable results of a state dominated from its inception by the interest of an Islamized and Arabized group. The form of the state that was created during the precolonial period, and consolidated and institutionalized its policies during the colonial and the postcolonial periods, laid the seeds of the current political violence. The legacies of slavery and colonialism have contributed to the invention of two categories of people with different entitlements. Those who are considered Arabs by the racialized state are treated as citizens and those who are perceived as non-Arabs are treated as subjects.

The political history of the Sudan has shown the relationship between the process of state formation and the construction of institutionalized and fixed racial identities that have led to tension and the spread of violence in the Sudan. The process of state formation in the Sudan was/is a violent process. From its inception in the sixteenth century, different groups with competing vision of histories and identities struggled over power, wealth, and identity of the state. Discrimination, displacement, and slavery were strategies used by the state to quell opposition. As I have argued in chapters 2 and 3, the legacy of slavery, the colonial policy of indirect rule, and the imposition of Arabization and Islamization have contributed to the unfolding crisis in the Sudan. The recent manifestation of the conflict in Darfur can be traced to the history of the state formation in the region. As O'Fahey states,

> Historically, Darfur was a sultanate, established in 1650 dominated by the Fur people from whom the ruling group emerged. However, the fur people ruled the kingdom with the support of elites from the major ethnic groups in the region. With the support of the state, the settled peoples, mainly non-Arab, were able to control the nomads until 1874. When the kingdom was restored in 1898 by Ali Dinar he spent most of his time driving the nomads, north and south of the settled area, back, until the British killed him in 1916. The British then discovered that they had no alternative but to continue his policy. They also kept the old ruling elite intact; many of the educated Darfurians of today descend from that elite.[12]

In the kingdom of Darfur, however, the process of state building relied on the labor of slaves.

> [S]laves were essential to the efficient functioning of the economic and political life of the state and to the administrative system that centered on the sultan. The procuring of the slaves was carried out either by the Arab cattle nomads of southern Darfur, the Baggara, or by raiding parties sponsored by the sultans.[13]

The use of slaves as agricultural laborers was common. Being a Muslim in Darfur did not protect many Muslims from being enslaved by the cattle nomads or the nobles of the kingdom. Slaves were also used in the army. However, as Douglas Johnson argues,

> The fact that the soldiers frequently became Muslim did not necessarily make them more free. Coming from the peripheries of a state thus defined one's status within the state. And in this respect territorial origin did become a factor in social stratification.[14]

Like the case of Southern Sudan, the practice of slavery and the slave trade in the region of Darfur created a racialized perception dividing the people of Darfur into Arab and non Arab/Black or *Zurga*. As the slave population in the North was obtained largely from southern and western regions, in the dominant Arabized and Islamized culture of the Central Sudan the terms "*abd*" or slave and black or *Zurga* were synonymous. Even Western Sudanese who become Muslims or exercised some power in the colonial and postcolonial state were stigmatized by their slave status or origins. Islam and the claim of Arab patrilineal descent in turn provided the ideological justification for the practice of racism and the use of violence. The practice of racialization and racism then makes color and religion irrelevant in the context of Darfur. Instead, it is descent or origin that matters. As in the case of the Southern Sudanese, those converted to Islam were not fully accepted into the society. They were not treated by the Arabized and Islamized state as citizens with social and political rights. According to Douglas Johnson, instead "[the] acceptance of Islam by the Sudanic kingdoms helped to sharpen the divide between the states and their hinterlands; between those who could claim the protection of law, and those without legal rights."[15]

Darfur experienced centralized political institution long before its formal incorporation into the colonially created "modern Sudan" in January 1, 1917.[16] However, the centralized kingdom governed through traditional political institutions such as local chiefs. Although these forms of political institutions prevented the development of a common sense of identity among the different groups in the region, agreed mechanisms such as chiefs' meetings were forged to deal with conflicts and tensions triggered by competition over resources and power. Local chiefs, religious leaders, and political elites from the region had convened a series of conferences in the past to lessen the tension between the two main groups—sedentary farmers such as the Fur, Masalit, and others, and cattle nomads, the Baqqara.[17] Indeed, these traditional mechanisms are deployed in many conflict situations in Africa and have been relatively successful in preventing the escalation of violence in multiethnic societies.

When the British incorporated Darfur in the modern Sudan in 1917, the precolonial traditional political and administrative institutions were kept in place. The colonial state introduced the policy of "native administration" in Darfur in the 1920s. Like the policy of indirect rule in Southern Sudan, the British administration encouraged people of Darfur to govern themselves according to their customs and traditions. In turn, the religious and tribal institutions were institutionalized and given more power. The native administration had the dual task of maintaining firm boundaries between different groups and of asserting authority within these communities. This colonial policy in turn maintained the precolonial legacies of slavery, racism, and discrimination. At the regional level, for instance, the region continued to witness the practice of slavery and the slave trade. At the national level, colonial policies led to the marginalization of the region economically and politically. As a result, many people from Darfur were forced to migrate to Central Sudan in search of employment in the cotton schemes due to lack of economic opportunities at home.

The postcolonial process of state building in the Sudan is characterized by violent confrontation and the marginalization of ethnic groups and regions. Even more than the eastern and the southern regions, the western region of Darfur has been neglected. Although the region of Darfur has contributed greatly to the national income through its cash crops and livestock, the agricultural and industrial developments of the Sudan are mainly concentrated in Central Sudan. Like the eastern, southern, and northern regions, the western region of Darfur suffers from a lack of social services in the areas of health and education. However, "[the] discontents in these regions have thus far largely been viewed as of secondary in importance to those of the South."[18] These realities of inequality and marginalization have been ignored and covered for decades under the rhetoric of common Arabic culture and Muslim faith. The people of Darfur have long attempted to challenge the government in Khartoum.[19] It was only in "the mid-1960s that some educated elites of Darfur, both Arab and non-Arab,"[20] began to participate in the national government, and to demand equal share of power and wealth. Moreover, those elites invoked their regional identity to assert their political claim.[21]

The tension between the various ethnic groups in Darfur has also been aggravated by the competition over scarce natural resources and the environmental changes that have affected the region since the 1980s. One of the causes of the current political violence dates back to the 1980s when a period of droughts accel-erated the desertification process in northern and central Darfur, which in turn led to much greater pressure on water and grazing resources as the camel nomads were forced to move southward. Conflicts over natural resources become bloodier and much more destructive when guns become easily available. Over the past two decades, the old balance between Arab nomads and non-Arab settled farmers has broken down, as Jeevan Vasagar indicates:

> In the past, the nomads would graze their goats and cattle in the north of Darfur during the rainy season, then move to the greener south during the dry season. After the rains, when the farmers had gathered in their crops, the nomads would tend their herds in the farmers' empty fields. As the population has grown, both sides have sought to buttress their way of life. Nomadic groups have sought farmland on which to settle, while farmers have started to keep their own herd of cattle. A conflict over resources was brewing, but it was political strategies that lit the spark.[22]

However, the political violence in Darfur became unmanageable when the government through its Arabized and Islamized policies began to arm, train, and support Arabic-speaking cattle nomads in the 1980s. The militarization of the crisis has grown ever since Sadiq al-Mahdi, the prime minister in the mid-1980s, made a decision to give arms to the Arabic-speaking cattle nomads, the Baqqara of southern Darfur, presumably to defend themselves against the Sudan People's Liberation Army (SPLA). In the beginning, the government's plan was to use the armed militia against the northern Dinka in an attempt to combat the SPLA's activities in the area. In its attacks against the northern Dinka, thousands were shot, tortured, killed, or mutilated. Others mainly women and children were taken as slaves.[23]

The racialization of the conflict, however, has grown rapidly since the Islamist regime of President Omer al-Bashir came to power by a military coup in 1989. Bashir's regime has attempted to impose the Arab and Islamic identity on all the people of the Sudan including the Muslim people of Darfur through its policy of *Jihad*—holy war. When the two rebel groups began their military operations in the region in early 2003, the government was doubtful about using the national army, because much of its rank and file is drawn from Darfur's Africans who might prove reluctant to fight their own people. Instead, Arab tribal leaders were encouraged to enlist men to the government's side. They were supplied with weapons and air support from helicopter gunships and Antonov bombers. And thus a program of systematic ethnic cleansing was unleashed.

The government forces and the *Janjaweed* militia then unleashed fear and terror among civilians in Darfur as Marc Lacey described:

> After the rebels struck last year, the government tapped into the Arab-African resentment that has long fostered here. The army began teaming its soldiers with the Janjaweed, who know no rules of war. The Janjaweed ride into villages as a group and begin

shooting anyone in sight. As the militiamen torch and loot, the villagers grab what they can and run.[24]

The policy of the state thus has led to the reproduction of an ideological and racist dimension, with each side—the killers and the victims—defining themselves as Arab and African respectively. The centuries old legacy of slavery was reproduced and redirected toward a specific group of people in Darfur presently categorized as African/black Muslims.

According to Alex de Waal, however, a combination of several factors has contributed to the growth of militia in the context of Sudan's civil war. They are: local disputes involving two or more groups; a deliberate military strategy by the government and the army to use local militias; economic deprivation and lack of economic opportunities during famine and drought periods; and national political aspiration associated with the interest of the political parties.[25] However, the SPLA/M has also contributed ideologically and militarily to the conflict in Darfur. Ideologically, the SPLA/M's concept of "New Sudan" encouraged other marginalized peoples including people in Darfur to liberate themselves from the hegemony of the postcolonial Arabized and Islamized state in the Sudan.[26] Militarily, the SPLA/M attempted to open a new military front in southern Darfur under the leadership of Daoud Bolad in 1991. It was at this time that the Arab militias, first called *murahalin*, now *janjaweed*, began to commit crimes of enslavement and ethnic cleansing against innocent civilians in southern and western regions. Like the case of Southern Sudan, the current government has employed the policy of armed militias against people of Darfur. The result is the killing of tens of thousands of civilians, and the displacement of more than a million people in Darfur and in the neighboring country of Chad. Thus, the state policy of terror is at the center of the current political violence in the region.

The Pitfalls of the North–South Paradigm
in the Peace Process

In 2002, the GOS and the SPLA/M signed a series of accords and agreements that set the Inter-Governmental Authority on Development (IGAD) peace process on track.[27] Both sides signed a framework agreement in Naivasha Kenya on May 26, 2004.[28] The signed protocols address the three outstanding issues of power sharing, the status of the three regions of Southern Kordofan, Nuba Mountains, and Blue Nile, and the status of Abyei. Both sides have yet to sign a comprehensive cease-fire agreement. The signed framework agreement is currently facing serious challenges due to the manner in which the conflict and the peace process have been perceived.[29] The IGAD's main strategy has been to focus on resolving Sudan's civil war within the north–south paradigm that led to the Mackakos Protocol of July 2002, which included provisions for self-determination and a continuance of *sharia* law to continue in the North.[30] However, the spread of political violence in Darfur proves that these regions share a problem: "the marginalization of peripheral regions and groups by successive governments in Khartoum."[31]

A major pitfall of the peace process stems from the existing strategy of the IGAD mediators, which has been to limit the negotiating parties to the GOS and SPLA/M. From a democratic perspective, the strategy of the mediators remains unconvincing, and with the spread of political violence in the Darfur and the obstruction of the GOS in the peace process, it has become essential to bring other actors into the peace process and, just as importantly, into a transitional national government.

The signed peace framework between the GOS and the SPLA/M has reproduced the colonial discourse on Sudan, which constructed the country into two distinct entities—the north, and the south. The content of the framework indeed resembles

the British colonial policy of indirect rule or the native administration, which institutionalized the undemocratic decentralized
system of governance in Southern Sudan in the 1930s. The negotiating parties have not addressed two fundamental historical and
political legacies embedded in the structure of the postcolonial
state in the Sudan. These are the legacies of the racialized state
and the ethnicization of Southern Sudan. Instead of addressing
these two fundamental elements of the crisis, the two parties have
agreed to carry out two contradictory tasks. First, the GOS and
the SPLA/M have agreed to reform the state in the north without
de-racializing it, in the sense that both sides have agreed to a sharing of power and wealth at the national level, while retaining the
sharia law as the sole legal system in the capital city, Khartoum.[32]
The implementation of the Islamic law in Khartoum violates the
human rights of many non-Muslims and Muslims who prefer to
be treated as citizens with full rights. Second, the two sides have
also promised to decolonize the south from the north without de-
ethnicizing it. The signed protocol has given people of Southern
Sudan the right to exercise the right of self-determination
after six years through a referendum in which they will choose
either to stay in a united Sudan or to opt for separation. However,
the agreement also considers the customary law as an alternative
for the *sharia* law in the south. Like the British colonial policy of
indirect rule, the implementation of a constructed customary law
gives more power to despotic traditional institutions such as local
chiefs. In turn, this constructed customary law will likely consoli-
date ethnic identities in Southern Sudan, which have for decades
engendered only tensions and bloody conflicts.

Thus, the fundamental task of the democratic transformation
seems to be completely ignored in the current peace process. The
outcome of this disjointed framework, in the long run, will be the
persistence of an undemocratic racialized state in the North and
the creation of a despotic/decentralized government in the South.

In both cases, there is a strong possibility for renewed political violence from within and without. As I have argued in chapters 2 and 3, Africanism and Arabism in the context of Sudan's civil war are expressions of political identities rather than cultural ones. They are produced by the policies of the state. The crisis in Darfur is a major challenge to academics, policy makers, and politicians to move away from the narrow, race/ethnic-based politics that they have embraced for so many decades.

For some marginalized groups in the North, the SPLA/M seems to be moving away from its commitment to a New Sudan, which involves a fundamental transformation of the racialized state, in favor of political partnership with the government at the very time that the Sudanese state faces a crisis of legitimacy and survival greater than at any time since independence. The SPLA/M, for instance, in its manifesto issued in 1983,[33] stated: "We are committed to the establishment of a NEW and democratic Sudan in which equality, freedom, economic and social justice and respect for human rights are not mere slogans but concrete realities." The current crisis in Darfur shows that many disaffected groups will not accept an outcome whereby the division of power and wealth is merely redivided among the GOS and the SPLA/M.

CHAPTER 6

BEYOND "RACE" AND "ETHNICITY": TOWARD A TRANSFORMATIVE DISCOURSE FOR DEMOCRATIC CITIZENSHIP

> To testify to a history of oppression is necessary but it is not sufficient unless that history is redirected into intellectual process and universalized to include all sufferers.
> —Said, "The Politics of Knowledge," p. 313

The crisis in Darfur and the pitfalls of the north–south peace process have raised serious question about the future of the democratic project in the Sudanese context. How can democratic citizenship be restored in the context of competing racial and ethnic identities? By the late 1980s, scholarly works on transition from authoritarian to democratic regimes in Africa were facing increased critique for their failure to grapple with the historical and political dimensions of democratization challenges.[1] In hindsight, blame can be placed on the previous decade's preoccupation with issues of institutional building that came at the expense of consideration of the existing competing visions of histories and identities in African societies. Contemporary scholarship on Africa's civil wars is concerned mainly with interaction between elites and with specific models of institutional arrangements conducive to democratic governance. Relationships between democratization of the state and the legacies of the past and its implications to the practice of democratic citizenship in Africa are largely understudied. As a result, many scholars and policy makers interested in the question of democratization in Africa in general, and the Sudan in particular, have made no effort to examine the relationship among histories, identities, and political conflicts in the region.

As I have argued in previous chapters, ethnic domination and the crisis of the postcolonial state is a product of the legacies of slavery, colonialism, and the racialized postcolonial state in the Sudan. The implication of historical and political processes is thus felt in the present political violence in southern and western regions of the Sudan. Like the colonial policy of indirect rule, ethnic or racial politics of regionalism seeks to institionalize ethnicity in the postcolonial conditions. This approach tends to conceptualize citizenship as a group's entitlements rather than individual rights. It also forced people to identify themselves in essenialized terms. Consequently, ethnic regionalism neither questions the existing ethnic identities nor transcends them.

The political history of the Sudan demonstrates that transition to democracy requires much more than building political institutions and the reforming of nondemocratic forms of exercising power.[2] Democratization requires changes not only in political institutions but also in the structure of the societies; that is, ethnicity and race, in the context of the Sudan, have to be perceived within their historical and political contexts. Both race and ethnicity are political identities produced by the process of state formation. The reform of the postcolonial state and the consolidation of democracy and peace require the transformation of these identities in a way that enhance the right of citizenship to all members of the society. The main challenge during the transition period to democracy, then, is to combine the political reform with the expansion of democratic practices and to forge a culture of citizenship at the societal level, recognizing individual rights across the entire spectrum of the diverse social, political, and cultural landscape of contemporary realities of the Sudan.

As I have argued in chapter 3, the historical development of the centralized/racialized state in the Sudan, however, has created different categories of people with different sets of rights and entitlements. Those groups considered citizens have historically enjoyed access to power and wealth. The state, in turn, comes to be perceived in their images as Arab-Islamic. On the other hand, those groups considered subjects such as people of Southern Sudan and some groups of Western Sudan have been subjected to cultural and physical violence through the policy of postcolonial state.

Power, privilege, and the ownership of property have always been unequally allocated since the formation of the centralized state in the Sudan.[3] In a social context stratified by class, gender, ethnicity, and race, those who benefited from the state institutions have historically been defined as Arabs, overwhelmingly upper class, and male. Consequently, it is within this unequal structure of power and privilege that national identity is defined and located. For instance, to be a "Sudanese" is by definition not to be a Southern Sudanese, Beja, or Fur. In other words, the dominant ideology of "Arabness" is central in precipitating the gross inequalities of race, gender, and class experienced by the majority of those Sudanese relegated to the status of subjects rather than citizens. Arabness has become the very center of the dominant criteria for national prestige, decision-making, authority, and even intellectual leadership in the Sudan. Consequently, citizenship has been used as a mechanism of exclusion in this historical and political context.

The 1948 Nationality Act of the Sudan, for instance, defined citizenship in terms of membership in ethnic groups living within the territorial boundaries established for the Anglo-Egyptian rule in 1898. This colonially created law of citizenship invented the category of "foreigners" or aliens in the Sudan. Thus, being born in the Sudan, even to parents born there, did not entitle a person to citizenship in the absence of the proper "ethnic identification."

In the postcolonial state, the dominant ruling groups continue to use the Nationality Act of 1948 to exclude large groups of people from the right to citizenship, in particular immigrants from west Africa who have settled in the Sudan since the 1930s. Furthermore, the Nationality Act has enabled the postcolonial state to pursue its policy of Arabization and Islamization. Jay O' Brien argues,

> In practice, it often became sufficient to be acknowledged as a member of an Arab tribe to be accorded the rights and privileges of citizenship. In contrast, admitting to (or some times even being suspected of) membership of an ethnic group thought to have originated in west Africa and generally regarded as not Sudanese, was often sufficient to disqualify a claim to Sudanese citizenship, even for people whose families and lineages had established themselves in what came to be Sudan well before British conquest.[4]

As I have discussed earlier, the spread of violence in the Sudan demonstrates the failure of the nationalist movement to transcend the racial and ethnic identities. In the postcolonial context, however, both the included and the excluded have not moved away from these constructed racial and ethnic identities. Both groups are imprisoned by the discourse of race and ethnicity. This is due to the centrality of Arabism within the dominant national discourse of identity, which is articulated by the state in the Sudan. In the Sudan, Arab and African are usually perceived as fixed, static, and always antagonistic social and cultural categories. Francis Deng, for instance, known for his liberal vision of national integration, tends to conceptualize race, "ethnicity," and "tribe" in an essentialist manner. Although Francis Deng has pointed out the role of Arabization and Islamization processes in shaping the Arab identity, he does not show how these two processes were initially reinforced by the racialized state, which in turn produced two competing political identities. For instance, he said,

> Arabization and Islamization led to the evolution of descent groups in the North bearing the names of their original founders—and sometimes associating themselves into tribes with the names of the dominant lineages. These genealogies have been known to be traced with many jumps or lacunae back to Arabia and where the Sudanese lineage is a politically or religiously leading one, back to the Prophet Mohammed, his relatives, his close associates, or his tribe, the Quraysh.[5]

Yet, in reality, race should be understood not as an entity grounded in some permanent biological differences between human beings. Rather, race should be perceived as "an unequal relationship between social categories, characterized by dominant and subordinate patterns of social interaction, and reinforced by the intricate patterns of public discourse, power and privilege within the economic, social, and political institutions of the state."[6] However, the dominant discourse on political violence and democratic transformation in the Sudan continues to search for answers within the colonial construct of ethnicity and race.

In the context of the Sudan, the politics of racial/ethnic identity have been expressed by two discourses: national integration and separation. The discourse on national integration is articulated in a firm belief in diversity and unity, and in the struggle to outlaw all legal barriers that prevent equal opportunities to all groups. This discourse is linked to the politics of forging a nation state of common interests, aimed at achieving national integration and democratic reforms within the context of the existing racialized state. This discourse neither questions the legitimacy of the racial/ethnic categories nor the existing racialized postcolonial state. In the context of the Sudan, Muddathir Abd Al-Rahim said,

> The North differs from the South in that it is predominately Muslim and Arab while the South is mainly "pagan" and only to a

much lesser extent either Muslim or Christian. This however (though it may correctly be regarded as an adequate ground for claiming a special status for the South within the framework of a United Sudan) does not constitute a sound argument for the splitting of the Sudan into two sovereign states. For the modern state, especially in Africa, is not and could not be founded on religion, racial or even cultural homogeneity but is based, above all, on the community of interests and objectives of peoples who, different though they may be in certain aspects, have, in the present age, met across continental and not merely tribal or regional boundaries.[7]

By contrast, the separatist discourse of racial identity is deeply skeptical of democratic transformation, assuming that racial categories are real and fundamentally significant, and that efforts to distribute power have to be structured along the boundaries of race or ethnicity. The discourse emphasizes the cultural and political unity of a group and seeks the establishment of a separate state for the oppressed group.

Some Southern Sudanese nationalists have also advocated the same argument. For instance, Aggrey Jaden, who was the head of a southern government in exile, in his speech at the Round Table Conference of 1965 argued that the Sudan is divided into Arab race in the "north" and African race in the "south":

> With this real division, there are in fact two Sudans and the most important thing is that there can never be basis of unity between the two. There is nothing in common between the various sections of the community; nobody of shared beliefs, no identity of interests, no local signs of unity and above all, the Sudan has failed to compose a single community. The Northern Sudanese claim for unity is based on historical accident and imposed political domination over the Southern Sudan . . .[8]

In the Sudan, this discourse perceives race and ethnicity as fundamentally a social category, that all Arabs are naturally racist, either for genetic, biological, or psychological reasons, and negates the

very idea of meaningful social, economic, and political transformation. Like the discourse of national integration, the separatists'
discourse tends also to perceive race and ethnicity as ahistorical,
rather than fluid and constantly subject to reconfiguration. For
instance, Dunstan Wai viewed the political conflict in the Sudan as
a conflict between two distinct races: Arab and "Negroid African."
He stated,

> In essence, it is a conflict of nationalism: one rooted in Africanism
> and other in Arabism. It is not as a mere case of ethnicity. The
> northern Sudanese view themselves as Arabs and whether their
> Arabness is more by acquisition than heredity is less of importance.
> Whereas the southern Sudanese feel themselves to be authentically
> Negroid Africans in every way.[9]

Deng D. Akol Ruay further argues that

> The south is African and Christian and looks to Black Africa for
> cultural inspiration and to the developed world for scientific and
> technological progress. The north is Arabized and Islamized and
> looks to the Middle East and Far East for cultural animation.[10]

Although the advocates of national integration and separation
in the Sudan seem to use different discourses, there is a similarity
between them. Both are informed by the notion that the essential
problem facing the oppressed people is the reality of race and ethnicity. On the one hand, those who call for national integration
seek power not to dismantle the boundaries of race and ethnicity
but to reform the state in such a way that preserves the rights of
the oppressed groups and gradually integrates them into the mainstream society, which is Arabized and Islamized.

On the other hand, the separatists believe that national
integration is unachievable, for the oppressor—Arabs—cannot be
trusted to dismantle these racial and ethnic barriers. Indeed, the

national integration discourse tends to prefer working within the colonially inherited state, influencing those in power to reform the state in a way that recognizes the diversity of the society. They also believe that democracy works best when it is truly pluralistic and inclusive, with the voices and interests of all racial and ethnic groups taken into consideration. The discourse of national integration is a strategy to conceal the postcolonial manifestations of racism, without changing the institutional structures of racism and inequality, which triggered the dynamics of Arab domination and oppression. However, this discourse has failed to come to terms with the widespread racism, economic, and social injustices inflicted upon the oppressed groups even during the democratic period.

The major weakness in the politics of the racial and ethnic identity perspective is that it is informed by the principle of group entitlement. The emphasis on group entitlements tends to ignore the common interests that might exist between different oppressed groups in the country or the region. Both discourses tend to overlook the relationship between racism and inequality; it tends to conceptualize racism as a kind of cultural residue rather than the logical consequence of institutional arrangement and power relations, reinforced by state policies. Although the advocates of both discourses struggled to destabilize race and ethnicity, they were themselves frequently imprisoned by the language and the logic of colonial thinking.

Transcending "Race" and "Ethnicity" in the Postcolonial Sudan

In the Sudan, the official version of national history was invented at the time of state-building and nationalist struggle. This version of national history tended to emphasis the integrity and unity of the state. Consequently, the history of enslavement, oppression, and forced displacement of people was denied and suppressed. In reactions to denial and political oppression and marginalization, the oppressed groups have embarked on the process of reconstructing their own histories and identities. The discourse not only locates the oppressed group at the center of the historical process, but also questions the dominant narrative of the national identity. This counter discourse of history, however, often essentialized and ethnicized the group identity and grounded it in a fixed and static cultural and ideological boundary. In the postcolonial context, both the history and the politics of these essentialized identities are removed from the realm of political debate. Thus, proposed solutions to the problem of civil wars between different groups come to be viewed only in ethnic and racial terms without taking into account its historical and political contexts.

In the postcolonial period, to ethnicize groups becomes an effective political mechanism of exclusion and inclusion within the existing racialized state in the Sudan. Thus, the interpretation of the past in the country is linked to the existence of competing visions of identities and expectations. Each group is demanding for its own imagined identity in the postcolonial context. However, the institutionalization of group rights in the Sudan tends to ignore the heterogeneity that exists in each group in terms of social and political interests.[11]

Eva Poluha, for instance, shows how both ethnic identitification and ethnic decentralization endanger the democratic process.

> Focus on one's own ethnic group to the exclusion of others is necessary in order to make demands in the name of the group. It entails enhancing the norms, values, virtue, history and homogeneity of one's own group. At the same time, by its own logic such behavior means repressing the rights of minorities, even within their own areas because there is no place on a majority ethnic group's agenda for minorities. As a consequence, the behavior

and discourse of those promoting their own culture becomes anti-democratic.[12]

Since many Sudanese view their identities through the lenses of race and ethnicity, it is challenging to argue that different ethnic or racial groups may have the same racial/ethnic identity imposed on them through the process of state formation. For instance, although Sudanese refugees in Egypt would all be labeled African in the Egyptian context, they come from different groups, such as the Dinka, the Nuer, the Bari, the Fur, the Nuba, and so on, and they have little in common in terms of languages, culture, ethnic traditions, and religious affiliation. Yet, they are all considered African racially, in the sense that they will share many of the pitfalls and prejudices built into the institutional norms of the dominant social and political structure for those defined as non-Arabs or Africans. Moreover, there is an absence of political unity between these groups, in part, because their political leaders are imprisoned ideologically by the colonial assumptions of the past.

Imagining New Identities for Democratic Citizenship

While the dominant Arabized and Islamized discourse in the Sudan has the capacity to silence marginalized groups, postcolonial discourse represents a challenge to reading history discursively. In this study, I question the usefulness of such concepts as African and Arab in the Sudanese context. Both concepts fundamentally justify colonialism. The significance of this is in the representations, which are ascribed to African and Arab respectively. In this manner, African and Arab exist as inventions not only in the colonial discourse but as inventions in the Sudanese context. This mode of thinking continues to dominate and haunt all discussion of conflict and peace in the country. Scholars have failed to examine the discourse within which these identities have been located. Therefore, my question is how can Sudanese free themselves from the shackles of a discourse that constructs such representations? The difficulties in this process can be traced to the manner in which colonial binaries, such as African/Arab and "inferior"/ "superior," are deployed. While it may be true that the colonial experience is by no means monolithic, the key problem many writers have in articulating the liberation project is that they essentialize identity. D.A. Masolo has highlighted this two-fold problem:

> First, that formerly colonized persons ought to have one view of the impact of colonialism behind which they ought to unite to overthrow it; second, that the overthrow of colonialism be replaced with another, liberated and assumedly authentic identity. So strong is the pull toward the objectivity of this identity that most of those who speak of Africa from this emancipatory perspective think of it only as a solid rock which has withstood all the storms of history except colonialism. Because of the deeply political gist of the colonial/postcolonial discourse, we have come to think of our identities as natural rather than imagined and politically driven.[13]

Unlike national integration, which seeks representation within the existing racialized state, or separation, which favors the construction of parallel ethnic or racial institutions controlled by the oppressed groups, transformative discourse mainly seeks the de-racialization of the state, de-ethnicization of society, and redistribution of resources along more egalitarian lines. Further, the transformative discourse seeks neither the integration nor the separation of the oppressed groups; rather, it seeks to deconstruct the ideological foundation, the social categories, and the institutional power of race and ethnicity in the Sudan. It advocates a restructuring of power relations and authority between groups and classes in such a way so as to make ethnicity/race irrelevant as social and political criterion for entitlement.

This new political discourse perceives racial identities as the product of both history and politics. Racial and ethnic identities, in the Sudan, are both the result and the consequences of struggle; they are dynamic and ever changing. For instance, the colonial and the postcolonial social and political history of the Southern Sudanese is, in part, the struggle to preserve their own group's sense of identity, social cohesion, and integrity, in reaction to policies that had been designed by the Arabized and Islamized state to deny them their common humanity and historical particularity.

However, the escalation of violence and the increased numbers of refugees to neighboring countries certainly led to some changes in people's perceptions about their ethnic and racial identities. In the case of Southern Sudanese, the conception of racial and ethnic categories is being questioned and transformed. The circumstances of displacement and refugeeness redefined what African and Arab meant in the Sudanese and exile contexts. Thus, the generalization and the rigid boundaries of racial and ethnic identities of the past no longer make much sense. Refugee experiences indicate that the liberation and democratization of the Sudan's societies involves the invention of new traditions and new communities, and not the glorification of an idealized past.

For the Southern Sudanese, however, race/ethnicity has come to mean an identity of survival and victimization, defined through oppression by those racial groups that exercise power and privilege. It is a political awareness of shared experience, suffering, and struggle against the barriers of racial and ethnic division. These collective experiences and memories form the basis of a historical and political consciousness in a postcolonial condition. This new distinct sense of racial or ethnic identity is imposed on the oppressed and yet represents a reconstructed critical memory of the group's collective historical grievances.

In the Sudan, many groups, such as the Dinka, the Fur, and the Beja, that have divergent ethnic and cultural attributes, speak various languages, and possess different cultures, now share common experiences of oppression and inequality due to the policy of the racialized state. However, there is an absence of unity between these oppressed groups, in part because their political leaders are imprisoned ideologically by the assumptions and realities of the past. For instance, in August 1991, some of SPLA/M's senior leaders such as Dr. Lam Akol Ajawin, a Shilluk, and Dr. Riak Machar, a Nuer, broke with the SPLA/M to form a splinter group known as the Nasir faction. The Nasir faction charged Dr. John Garang with dictatorial rule and human rights violations. The group also argued that Garang did not call for secession for the south. The ethnic war within the civil war that pitted Dinka against Nuer proved to be as brutal as that between the once united SPLA and government forces.[14] These leaders have not questioned the past of the present, mainly, the legacy of slavery, the colonial policy and the nature of the existing racialized state. These legacies have produced the logic of inferiority and racial inequality, which sees the people of Southern Sudan and others groups from western and eastern regions as permanent subjects and the Arab as the eternal symbols of power, privilege, and wealth.

One of the major political developments in the postcolonial political history of the Sudan is the introduction of the notion of a New Sudan or "Sudanism" by the SPLA/M. This new transformative discourse shifts the discussion on Sudan's conflict from race and ethnicity to issues of nationality and citizenship. John Garang argues,

> SPLM/A is committed to solving the nationality and religion questions, to the satisfaction of all the Sudanese citizens and with a democratic and a secular context and in accordance with

the objective reality of our country . . . the nationality question is something that must be discussed. We are an Arab country, we are an African country. Are we a hybrid? Are we Afro-Arab, are we what?[15]

This new notion attempts to redefine and restructure the framework of national identity, in the Sudan. It rejects the existence of a single vision of national identity, which historically meant being associated with the Arab-Islamic heritage. Instead, it sees the cultural identity of the country as essentially a product of historical development and argues that

Its African and Arab identity factors, their respective cultures in addition to Islam, Christianity and other traditional beliefs some of the citizens observe and practice, are influences that do not exist in isolation from each other. These are elements which over the ages have been inextricably interwoven into the fabric of our society. They are strands that have been used together to form an integral whole that cannot be represented or denoted by any one particular constituent element . . . the diverse nationalities making up Sudan can and will have to coalesce—into a Sudanese nation (National Formation) with its own distinct civilization and with the capacity to contribute in its own right to the enrichment of human civilization rather than merely serve as an appendage of other nations.[16]

Unlike the earlier Southern Sudanese nationalists of the 1960s, who demanded the construction of a new state in the South, the SPLA/M came to the realization that racial and ethnic inequality cannot be abolished unless the basic power structures of society are transformed. This requires, in turn, the establishment of a broad coalition between people of Southern Sudan and other groups who experience oppression and social and economic inequality. Through the long history of struggle against oppression, marginalization, and racial discrimination, the SPLA/M articulates a new vision of identity for a more humane society, one in which the rights of the individual are inclusive and based on the fact of citizenship. By doing so, the SPLA/M seeks to change the political culture of the Sudan from a racialized discourse and analysis to a critique of oppression, inequality, and injustice. This approach could have widespread appeal to the majority of people in the Sudan. Recently, in the context of Darfur's crisis, the Sudan Liberation Movement/Army (SLM/A) has also used the notion of Sudanism in its political declaration. It stated,

> The SLM/A shall struggle to realize a new system of rule that fully respects the cultural diversity in the Sudan and creates new democratic conditions for cultural dialogue and cross-fertilization generating a new view of the Sudanese identity based on Sudanism. Sudanism will provide the Sudanese with the necessary space, regardless of whether they are Arabs or Africans, Christians or Muslims, Westerners or Easterners, Southerners or Northerners to achieve greater cohesiveness on the basis of the simple fact of being Sudanese.[17]

Democratic citizenship, therefore, requires a transformative political discourse that goes beyond race and ethnicity. The recent conflict in Darfur, as Francis Deng argues,

> [S]ignifies a nation in painful search of itself and striving to be free from any discrimination due to race, ethnicity, religion or culture in any region. In view of this pervasive challenge, the country is called upon to transform itself and forge a new common and inclusive framework of national identity in which all Sudanese would find a sense of belonging as citizens with equality and dignity of citizenship.[18]

Given these historical and political legacies, any attempt to end political violence will have to confront the nature of the racialized state. Without de-racializing the state in a way that transcends the dichotomies into a national framework reflecting the multiplicity of histories and identities, it is ultimately impossible to end the human tragedy and to reconstruct a new postcolonial state based on citizenship.

CONCLUSION

Contemporary scholarship on political violence and civil wars in Africa has focused either on the colonial or the postcolonial periods. Very little exists on precolonial histories. Consequently, the political violence in the Sudan, for instance, is often conceptualized in essentially ethnic and religious terms. This inadequate perspective has led many policy makers and scholars to propose liberal democracy and ethnic or regional arrangements as a solution to the crisis of citizenship in postcolonial Africa.

The study rejects the premise that violent conflict in the Sudan is a result of deep ancient hatreds and ethnic loyalties. Instead, the crisis of the postcolonial state and the spread of political violence in the Sudan can be understood as a critique of the postcolonial state. This crisis, however, can be explained only by locating the precolonial and the colonial in a postcolonial context. It is the racialized state that transformed cultural identities into political identities through the practice of slavery in the precolonial period, indirect rule during the colonial period, and an exclusive policy of citizenship in the postcolonial period. Moreover, the study acknowledges the centrality of the historical legacy of slavery and colonialism in the crisis of postcolonial citizenship in the region. The political history of the Sudan suggests the need to question and problematize the conventional wisdom about democracy and peace in multiethnic and cultural setting. The racialized and despotic state in the Sudan has had a crucial historical role in spreading political violence in the southern, eastern, and western regions.

Indeed, the kind of state that has emerged in the Sudan since the sixteenth century has created groups of people with inferior status in relation to the state. The initial process of state formation relied on violence as a mechanism of both conquest and consolidation of the state power. Consequently, the survival of the state seems to rely on its ability to perpetuate violence and oppression against the colonized peoples, who are treated as subjects rather than citizens. In the Sudan, a precolonial legacy of enslavement laid the seeds for the creation of two competing racialized identities, which were strengthened by the British colonial policy toward Southern Sudan. Whereas Arabism was a product of the practice of enslavement, Africanism was a product of the colonial policy of indirect rule. The colonial policy of indirect rule not only invented the African identity in the Southern Sudan, but also fragmented it into conflicting political communities in the form of ethnicities.

Like the people of Southern Sudan, the Fur and the people from the Nuba Mountains were subjected to the practices of slavery and colonialism. These groups were treated as subjects rather than citizens and assigned inferior racial identities in the existing Arabized and Islamized state. The construction of ethnic, racial, or regional identities in the Sudan is inherently linked to the processes of state formation in the region. These political and racial identities were created in the Sudan to assign and perpetuate inferior status to some groups, while others were allowed access to privilege, power, and wealth. In the end, their political creation produced particular forms of power and exclusion.

The nature of the process of state formation not only transformed structures of societies, but also conditioned the form of resistance to the colonial and the postcolonial state. The process of state formation during the colonial period had contributed to economic and political inequalities between various ethnic groups in the Sudan. Coupled with the institutionalization of ethnic identity as a criterion for economic, social, and political entitlements, the realization of inclusive citizenship in the postcolonial period has become impossible. In the postcolonial context, the dominant political discourse in the Sudan has been structured by the existence of colonially created political and racial identities. Neither the colonizers nor the colonized have questioned the historical and political legitimacy of these racial and political identities. African versus Arab in the Sudan is perceived as given and unhistorical. Consequently, no efforts have been made to transcend these racial identities in a way that could have institutionalized citizenship instead of ethnic, racial, or regional entitlements in the postcolonial state.

However, the changes that occurred in people's perceptions as a result of war, displacement, and immigration require that political leaders reach out to other oppressed sectors of society, creating a common political platform for political, economic, and social justice. Political leaders among the Southern Sudanese and the people of Darfur, for instance, must also look outward, embracing those oppressed groups of different ethnic or racial backgrounds who share a vision of democratic citizenship. Thus, the major challenge for the oppressed groups is to construct a transformative framework for democratic citizenship that eliminates the dualism between subjects and citizens that was institutionalized during the colonial period. But this cannot be done unless these groups construct a new discourse of liberation that transcends the colonial boundaries of a singular ethnic/racial identity and embraces a vision of democratic citizenship that could address the past. It is important, therefore, to move beyond the confines of such racial and ethnic identities that claim, for example, that only the Southern Sudanese or the Fur are Africans or that the Baqqara or Ja'aliyyun are Arabs. These essentialized racial and ethnic identities indeed are constraints rather than a practical option for resistance and liberation in postcolonial conditions.

Indeed, faced with a deepening crisis of the postcolonial state and the growing discontentment in the eastern and western regions, only a de-racialized democratic regime can be expected to confront the grievances that gave rise to war in the south and are producing conflict in other parts of the country, particularly in Darfur. If the Sudanese political forces, in particular the SPLA/M and the GOS continue to ignore these historical and political realities and view the peace process merely in terms of north and south, Arab and African, then it is predictable that the Sudan's crisis will deepen and violence will continue.

Notes

Preface

1. See my previous work (2001) Sudan's Civil War.

Introduction

1. The government backed militia, known as *Janjaweed*, engaged in what United Nations officials described "as ethnic cleansing of the African ethnic groups of Darfur." Men have been summarily executed, women have been raped, and more than 100,000 have been forced into exile to neighboring countries, and more than 30,000 have been killed. For more details see Office of UN Resident and Humanitarian Coordinator for the Sudan (2004) "A Briefing Paper on the Darfur Crisis: Ethnic Cleansing," March 25.
2. Zartman, *Collapsed State*; Ake, *Democracy and Development in Africa*; Davidson, *The Black Man's Burden*; Chabal, *Political Domination in Africa*; Chris Allen, "Warfare, Endemic Violence, and State Collapse in Africa," pp. 367–384; Reno, *Warlord Politics and African States*; Bayart, *The State in Africa*; Callaghy, *State-Society Struggle*.
3. Callaghy, "Politics and Vision in Africa"; Ake, "Explaining Political Instability in New State," pp. 247–259; Zolberg, "The Structure of Political Conflict," pp. 70–87; Diamond, "Introduction: Roots of Failure, Seeds of Hope."
4. For a unique perspective on relationships between the colonial state and the legalization of political identities in Africa see Mamdani, *Citizen and Subject*.
5. Baker, "The Class of 1990," pp. 115–127.
6. Bratton and Van de Walle, "Neopatrimorial Regimes and Political Transition in Africa," pp. 453–489; Bratton, *Democratic Experiments in Africa*; Fredman, "Agreeing to Differ," pp. 829–858;

Haggard and Kufman, *The Political Economy of Democratic Transitions*; Hyden, Olowu and Okoth-Ogendo, *African Perspectives on Governance*; Joseph, "Democratization in Africa after 1989," pp. 363–382.

7. For an interesting discussion on the relationship between state and society from African perspectives see Chole and Ibrahim, *Democratization Processes in Africa*; Mamdani, "Democratic Theory and Democratic Struggle"; Mamdani, "Indirect Rule, Civil Society, and Ethnicity," pp. 145–151; Sachikonye, *Democracy, Civil Society and the State*.

8. An-Naim, "The National Question of Constitutionalism"; Salih, "The Sudan, 1985–1989," pp. 199–224; Lesch, *The Sudan*; Salih and Markakis, *Ethnicity and the State in Eastern Africa*; Poluha, *Ethnicity and Democracy*, pp. 30–41; Woodward and Murray, *Conflict and Peace*.

9. For an interesting study on issues of state, history, identity, and conflict in northeast Africa, see Jalata, *State Crises, Globalization and National Movements*.

10. See Mamdani, *Citizen and Subject*.

11. Some of the main works in this area are written by Austen, "From the Atlantic to the Indian Ocean"; see also Eltis and Richardson, "West Africa and the Transatlantic Slave Trade," pp. 16–35; and Eltis, "The British Contribution," pp. 211–229; Cooper, *Plantation Slavery*; and Lovejoy, *The Ideology of Slavery in Africa*; Miers and Roberts, *The End of Slavery in Africa*; John Ralph Willis, ed. (1985) *Slaves and Slavery in Muslim Africa*, London: Frank Cass; see also Alpers, *Ivory and Slaves*; Klein, *The Middle Passage*; Sikainga, *Slaves into Workers*.

12. Alier, *Southern Sudan*.

13. For a general survey of these dominant conventional writings see Bashir, *The Southern Sudan*. For perspectives from Southern Sudan see Deng and Oduho, *The People of Southern Sudan*; see also Wai, *The Southern Sudan*.

14. But rather than focusing on the history of the refugee communities, this study examines the processes that influence its formation and the contexts which structure the emergence of a new sense of cultural and political identities.

Chapter 1 Reconceptualizing History, Identity, and Conflict

1. See, for instance, Deng, *War of Visions*; Lesch, *Contested National Identities*; El-Affendi, "Discovering the South," pp. 371–389; Markakis, *National and Class Conflict*; Douglas Johnson (2003) *The Root Causes of Sudan's Civil Wars*, Oxford: James Currey; Bloomington: Indiana University Press.
2. For an interesting discussion see Paris, "Peacebuilding and the Limits of Liberal Internationalism," pp. 54–89.
3. For examples, countries such as Rwanda, Angola, Namibia and Mozambique, Ethiopia, and Sudan have experienced some forms of unsuccessful democratic transitions. For an interesting discussion on the problems of democratization in war-torn societies, see Ottaway, "Democratization in Collapsed States," in Zartman, *Collapsed States*; also see Idris, "The Racialized and Islamicised Sudanese State."
4. Said Adejumobi, "Citizenship, Rights, and the Problem of Conflicts," p. 170.
5. Woodword, *Sudan: 1898–1989*.
6. See Hassan, *The Arab and the Sudan*.
7. For some work by Southern Sudanese see, for example, Deng and Oduho, *The Problem of the Southern Sudan*; Albino, *The Sudan*; Malwal, *People and Power in the Sudan*.
8. See, for instance, Ruth McCreery (1946) "Moslems and Pagans of the Anglo-Egyptian Sudan," *The Moslem World*, vol. xxxvi, pp. 252–260.
9. The colonial discourse on Africa tends to divide Africa into two distinct regions in terms of race, culture, and history—"North Africa" and "Black Africa."
10. See Mamdani, *When Victims Become Killers*, ch. 1.
11. For an interesting work on the relationship between history and identity see Sorenson, "History and Identity in the Horn of Africa," pp. 227–252.
12. See, for instance, Anderson, *Imagined Communities*.
13. See work by Althusser, *Lenin and Philosophy*.
14. Anderson, *Imagined Communities*.

15. Hobsbawm and Ranger, *The Invention of Tradition*.
16. See Mamdani, *Citizen and Subject*, and his work "Indirect Rule, Civil Society, and Ethnicity," pp. 145–151.
17. See Said, "Civil Wars in Africa," p. 160.
18. See Johnson, *The Root Causes*, p. 7.

Chapter 2   Slavery, Colonialism, and State Formation in the Sudan

1. Brenner, *The Shehus of Kukawa*, p. 115.
2. Al Tunisi, *Voyage*, pp. 33–34.
3. Collins, *Land Beyond the Rivers*, p. 225; see also his work "The Nilotic Slave Trade: Past and Present," pp. 140–161.
4. O'Fahey and Spaulding, *Kingdoms of the Sudan*, p. 82.
5. Cordell, *Dar al-Kuti and Last Years of Trans-Saharan Slave Trade*, p. 79.
6. Indeed, Islam also played a significant role in the conduct of military operations. Muslim soldiers prayed before combat and attempted to visualize through prayer who the winner would be, always believing that Allah would intervene on their behalf, and that death in war would assure them heaven.
7. Adams, *Nubia*, p. 12.
8. Ibrahim, *The Shaiqiya*, p. 8.
9. Arab invasion of the Sudan in the ninth century resulted in the intermarriage of Arabs and the indigenous peoples. In the nineteenth century, Northern Sudan's cultural norms, social organizations, and languages of most people in this part of the Sudan were Arabic. For more details see Hassan, *The Arabs and the Sudan*.
10. Johnson, *The Root Causes*, p. 2.
11. See O'Fahey and Spaulding, *Kingdoms of the Sudan*, ch. iv.
12. See Sikainga, *Slaves into Workers*; also see Spaulding, *The Heroic Age in Sinnar*.
13. See McLoughlin, "Economic Development," pp. 355–389.
14. According to Islam, the only legal way for enslaving a person was that he or she was a non-Muslim who was captured in the course of *jihad*—holy war. For more details, see Hunwick, "Black Africans in the Islamic World," pp. 5–37.
15. See Idris, *Sudan's Civil War*, ch. 2.

16. See Hassan, *The Arabs and the Sudan*; and also see MacMichael, *A History of the Arabs in the Sudan*.
17. Passmore and Sanderson, *Education, Religion and Politics in Southern Sudan*, p. 8.
18. See Idris, *Sudan's Civil War*, ch. 2.
19. Johnson, *The Root Causes*, p. 5.
20. See Gray, *A History of Southern Sudan*.
21. Johnson, *The Root Causes*, p. 60.
22. Cited in T.D. Murray and A.S. White (1895) *Sir Samuel Baker: A Memoir*, London: Macmillan, p. 138.
23. See Bjorkelo, *Prelude to the Mahdiyya*.
24. The *Jellaba* are a group of Arabized Sudanese, mainly resident in the North-Central Sudan but active all over the country, who have benefited from such activities as trade, including the slave trade, and acted as auxiliaries to successive colonial and postcolonial regimes. For more details on the development of this group, see Kok, "Sudan: Between Radical Restructuring and Deconstruction of State System," pp. 555–561.
25. Willis, *Slaves and Slavery in Muslim Africa*, p. 16.
26. See Jalata, *State Crises, Globalization and National Movements in North-East Africa*, p. 22.
27. The word "*Fallata*" (slave) is a derogatory term widely used in the north to refer to people who came from Western Africa and the Western Sudan.
28. Ewald, *Soldiers, Traders, and Slaves*, p. 176.
29. Idris, *Sudan's Civil War*, ch. 2.
30. McLoughlin, "Economic Development," pp. 355–389.
31. For an interesting work, see Sikainga, *Slaves into Workers*.
32. Warburg, "Slavery and Labor in the Anglo-Egyptian Sudan," p. 232.
33. Makris, "Construction of Categories from the era of Colonialism."
34. One of the strong supporters of domestic slavery in the Sudan was Slatin Pasha, until 1914 the Sudan's inspector general. For more details see Warburg, "Slavery and Labor in the Anglo-Egyptian Sudan," pp. 221–244.
35. See Willis, "Report on Slavery," p. 18.
36. See a memorandum prepared on the request of Wingate, cited in Cromer to Salisbury.
37. Howell, "Politics in the Southern Sudan," pp. 163–164.

38. For the full text of the Condominium Agreement, see Abd Al-Rahim, *Imperialism and Nationalism in the Sudan*, pp. 133–135.
39. Cited in Lavin, *The Condominium Remembered*, p. 20.
40. Kitchener, "Memorandum to Mudirs," enclosed in Cromer to Salisbury.
41. Cited in Mair, *Native Policies in Africa*, p. 181.
42. Daly, *British Administration and the Northern Sudan*, p. 168.
43. See Charles L. (1918) *Native Races and Their Rulers*, Cape Town, Argus Printing, p. 30.
44. A letter to the Finacial Secretary, 29/3/22, SGA, civSEC 20/21/97.
45. MacMichael, *The Anglo-Egyptian Sudan*, p. 240.
46. See E.E. Evans-Pritchard (1938) *Administrative Problems in the Southern Sudan*, Oxford: Oxford University Summer School on Colonial Administration, p. 77.
47. See his letter to the Civil Secretary on "Nuer Policy."
48. The Closed Districts Ordinance was designed to end the slave trade. The areas, that were closed were the ones in which the non-Arab groups (the objects of slaveholders) lived.
49. See "General Statement of Policy in the Southern Sudan with regards to administration, religion, and education."
50. See *Sudan Gazatte*, no. 402, 15/101/22.
51. See Memorandum on Southern Policy, by Sir Harold MacMichael, Bahr al Ghazal 1/1/1.
52. Johnson, *The Root Causes*, p. 13.
53. See Robert Collins (1964) "Autocracy and Democracy in the Southern Sudan: The Rise and Fall of the Chiefs' Court," in A. Rivkin, ed., *Nations by Design*, New York: Anchor Book.
54. For instance, the Rajaf Language Conference of 1928 recommended the adoption of some indigenous languages in schools namely Bari, Dinka, Moro, Ndogo, Nuer, Shilluk, Zande, etc.
55. See Daly, British Administration and the Northern Sudan, p. 188.

Chapter 3   Nationalism, State, and Identity Politics

1. Newbury, "Background to Genocide: Rwanda," pp. 12–17.
2. Apter, *Rethinking Development*, p. 40.

3. See Dunstan Wai's work (1984) in *Issue: A Journal of Africanist Opinion*, 13, p. 9.
4. *Southern Sudan Vision*, April 1, 1992.
5. See El-Affendi, "Discovering the South," p. 373.
6. Ibid., p. 373.
7. Idris, *Sudan's Civil war*, ch. 4.
8. For more details see Powell, "Colonized Colonisers, Egyptian Nationalists and the issue of the Sudan, 1875–1919," pp. 240–241.
9. Cited in Douglas Johnson, ed. (1998) *British Documents on the End of Empire: Sudan, Part 1, 1942–1950*, London: HMSO, see pp. 234–235; also see *Hadarat al Sudan*, June 25, 1924.
10. For a detailed study see Khalid, *The Government They Deserve*.
11. Idris, *Sudan's Civil War*, p. 102.
12. See Keith Kyle (1966) "The Southern Problem in the Sudan," *World Today*, 22, p. 513.
13. For more details, see Deng and Oduho, *The People of Southern Sudan*.
14. Kyle, "The Southern Problem in the Sudan," p. 513.
15. McClintock, "The South Sudan Problem," p. 467.
16. Badal, "The Rise and Fall of Separatism in South Sudan," pp. 463–474.
17. Ibid., p. 74.
18. Albino, *The Sudan,* p. 40.
19. Woodward, "Nationalism and Opposition in Sudan," pp. 381–382.
20. See Ali and Matthews, "Civil War and Failed Peace Efforts in Sudan."
21. See Garang, "The Shaping of a New Sudan," pp. 6–16.
22. See Abdel Salam, "Ethnic Politics in the Sudan," p. 61.
23. For the spread of violence and the failure of democracy during the civilian regime of Sadiq El Mahdi, see Anderson, *Sudan in Crisis*.
24. For a recent study on contemporary slavery in the Sudan, see Jok, *War and Slavery in Sudan*; also see Africa Watch (1990) *Denying the Honor of Living: Sudan A Human Rights Disaster*, New York: Africa Watch, Human Rights Watch.
25. *Southern Sudan Vision*, no. 2, November 20, 1992.
26. Ibid.
27. See Idris, "Sudan," p. 38.
28. See Mahgoub, *Democracy on Trial*, p. 206.

Chapter 4   Exile, Identity, and
Political Reform

1. From an appeal letter prepared by chiefs and elders of Equatoria region to Southern Sudanese abroad. These chiefs represented Juba, Yei, and Kaji Kaji counties in the SPLA/M controlled areas of Southern Sudan. The appeal letter urged for reconciliation, unity, and the need for general moblization. See *Sudan Democratic Gazette*, November, 1996.
2. From an interview with Achebe, cited in Appiah, *In My Father's House*, p. 137.
3. Sudanese refugees represent the largest foreign community in Egypt. The Egyptian government estimated the number of Sudanese in Egypt as 3 million, other conservative sources estimate between 200,000 to 300,000 Sudanese. For more details, see Sudan Cultural Digest Project (1996) "Coping With Dynamics of Culture and Change: The Case of Displaced Sudanese in Egypt," *Research Report*, no. 1, December.
4. As a result of this decree, the United Nations High Commission for Refugees (UNHCR) office in Cairo began to process Sudanese asylum cases.
5. From a letter of introduction of the Elderly Advisory Committee of Southern Sudan (EACOSS), n.d.
6. Interviewed on November 15, 1996.
7. Interviewed on November 23, 1996.
8. Interviewed on December 6, 1996.
9. Chambers, *Migrancy Culture Identity*, pp. 24–25; see also Cohen, *Global Diasporas,* p. 133.
10. See Sarap, "Home and Identity," p. 96.
11. Said, *Culture and Imperialism*, p. 216.
12. Ibid., p. 332.
13. Here, I mean by Southern Sudan the historical south that consists of the three provinces of Upper Nile, Equatoria, and Bahr al Ghazal. These three provinces differ historically from other marginalized areas of the Western, Eastern, and Central Sudan.
14. The use of the word identity in singular in this study should not be considered the negation of the multiplicity of Southern Sudanese experiences.

15. Interviewed on September 26, 1996.
16. See Alonso, "The Politics of Space, Time and Substance," pp. 379–405.
17. Interviewed on October 11, 1996.
18. See Deng, "Egypt's Dilemmas on the Sudan," pp. 50–56.
19. Interviewed on October 26, 1996.
20. Interviewed on September 30, 1996.
21. Interviewed on September 27, 1996.
22. Interviewed on September 28, 1996.
23. For a detailed historical study on this issue see Sharkey, *Living with Colonialism.*
24. Interviewed on October 3, 1996.
25. Some of these languages were Bari, Nuer, Dinka, Moru, Shilluk, and Azande among others.
26. From an interview with the Secretary of Finance, October 20, 1996.
27. The name is dedicated to the memory of Bishop Daniel Comboni.
28. See "Sudan: Church Grows Despite Severe Hardships," *Christianity Today* (1994) vol. 38, no. 4, April 4; [also see Hugh McCullum, pp. 12–16 (1995) "New Sudan Council of Churches," *One World* (206), June].
29. For detailed information see Edward's paper, "Southern Sudanese Informal Groups."
30. Interviewed on November 7, 1996.
31. See Deng, *War of Visions*, p. 190.
32. See African Rights (1995) "Great Expectations: The Civil Roles of the Churches in Southern Sudan," Discussion Paper, No. 6, April, London.
33. Interviewed on June 15, 1997.
34. Quoted from EACOSS letter, pp. 1–2.
35. Whereas the Arab league and the OAU voice support and outrage about what was happening in Bosnia and Somalia respectively, they are completely blind to the atrocities committed by the Islamic government of the Sudan against people of Southern Sudan.
36. Interviewed on July 18, 1997.
37. Interviewed on December 4, 1996.
38. In 1994, the SPLA/M held its first National Convention Conference in the south in which delegates had agreed to establish

civic authorities in the liberated areas in Southern Sudan. This new policy has given the SPLA/M credibility that encouraged civilian participation.

39. See Jok and Hutchinson, "Sudan's Prolonged Second Civil War," pp. 125–145.
40. Interviewed on October 11, 1996.
41. Interviewed on July 18, 1997.
42. The new political definition of the Southern Sudan includes also Abyei, the Nuba Mountains, and the Ingessena Hills. It rejects the colonially created border of Southern Sudan.
43. See the NDA, *Documents of the Conference on Fundamental Issues*, June 12–23.
44. Interviewed on July 30, 1997.
45. See Nyaba, *The Politics of Liberation in South Sudan*, p. 174.
46. Interviewed on June 20, 1997.
47. Interviewed on November 1, 1996.
48. There is a growing tendency among Southern Sudanese women to reject the conventions of the past and inventing new community structures and attitudes that legitimize their emerging new social and political visions in exile. For an interesting study see Edward, "Southern Sudanese Refugee Women," pp. 272–289.

Chapter 5   The Crisis in Darfur and the North–South Peace Process

1. See the Political Declaration of the Sudan Liberation Movement and Sudan Liberation Army (SLM/A), signed by Minni Arkou Minnawi, Secretary General, March 13, 2003, Darfur, Sudan, p. 2.
2. The term *Janjaweed* in the local context means outlaws—those who steal cattle. Some believe the word comes from Arabic—*jinn* for demon and *jawad* for horse. However, in the context of the current conflict in Darfur, the *Janjaweed* is the creation of Khartoum's government as Rwanda's *Interahamwe* was a creation of political elites.
3. See U.S. Secretary of State Colin L. Powell's remarks on the crisis in Darfur before the Senate Foreign Relations Committee, Washington DC, September 9, 2004.
4. See Susan Rice and Gayle Smith, *Washington Post*, May 30, 2004.
5. *The Globe and Mail*, Saturday, June 5, 2004, p. F4.

6. *Toronto Star*, July 9, 2004.
7. There were many songs against the *Zurga*—a term for "black Africans." For instance, in one of the *Janjaweed*'s camps, the recruits sang in Arabic: "We go to war, we go to defeat the rebels— we are the original people of this area." See Jeevan Vasagar, "Inside the Janjaweed: How One Man Escaped the Ethnic Cleansing in Darfur," *The Observer*, August 1, 2004.
8. See *Daily Star*, May 12, 2004.
9. See R.S. O'Fahey (2004) "A Distant Genocide in Darfur," *Sudan Studies Association Newsletter*, vol. 23, no. 1, May, p. 6.
10. *The Observer*, Sunday, May 30, 2004.
11. See Julie Flint (2004) "Shameful Muslim Silence on Darfur," *The Daily Star*, Wednesday, May 12.
12. O'Fahey, *A Distant Genocide in Darfur*, p. 6.
13. See R.S. O'Fahey (1973) "Slavery and the Slave Trade in Dar Fur," *Journal of African History*, vol. xiv, no. 1, p. 37.
14. Johnson, *The Root Causes*, p. 4.
15. Ibid., p. 3.
16. Ali Dinar, the last sultan of Darfur, was killed by the British troops of the Anglo-Egyptian Sudan on November 6, 1916.
17. See Alex de Waal (2004) "Darfur's Deep Grievances Defy All Hopes for an Easy Solution," *The Observer*, Sunday, July 25.
18. See "Sudan's Other Wars," Africa Briefing, Overview, International Crisis Group, June 25, 2003. Published in http://www.crisisweb. org/home/index
19. For instance, in 1991, the SPLA sent an armed force to Darfur led by Daoud Bolad to begin a liberation war against the government in the western region. Daoud Bold was a member of the National Islamic Front (NIF) who was disillusioned with the Islamist project after the failure of the government to address the historical grievances of his people in Darfur. Daoud was caught and killed by his former Islamist colleagues. Presently, some SLA/M members see their struggle as a continuation of Daoud's struggle.
20. See O'Fahey, *A Distant Genocide*, p. 6.
21. For an interesting work written on issues of racism, identity, and Islam in the context of Darfur, see Sharif Harir (1993) "Racism in Islamic Disguise? Retreating Nationalism and Upsurging Ethnicity in Dar Fur, Sudan," paper presented at a conference on the prospect of democracy in Sudan, Sudanese Studies Center, Cairo, Egypt.

22. *The Observer*, August 1, 2004.
23. See Jok, *War and Slavery.*
24. See Lacey, *New York Times*, May 4, 2004.
25. See de Waal (1993) "Some Comments on Militias in the Contemporary Sudan," in *Civil War in the Sudan*, p. 143.
26. In response to the government's policy of discrimination and ethnic cleansing, the non-Arab groups have also mobilized, adopting the term African, which helps to gain solidarity with the south based SPLA.
27. See IGAD Secretariat on Peace in the Sudan, Machakos Protocol, Machakos, Kenya, July 20, 2002.
28. Protocol Between the GOS and the SPLM on Power Sharing; Protocol Between the GOS and the SPLM/A on the Resolution of Abyei Conflict; Protocol Between the GOS and the SPLM on the Resolution of Conflict in Southern Kordofan/Nuba Mountains and Blue Nile States; Protocol Between the GOS and the SPLM on Wealth Sharing. All these protocols were signed in Naivasha, Kenya, May 26, 2004.
29. Some argue that the current peace negotiations in Kenya between the (GOS) and the (SPLA/M) is fueling the ethnic cleansing in Darfur, in the sense that the non-Arab groups feel that they are being left out, while the government is trying to use Arab nomads to keep control of the region.
30. See "Sudan's Other Wars" (2003) Africa Briefing, Overview, International Crisis Group, Brussels, June 25. Published in http:// www.crisisweb.org/ home/index
31. Ibid.
32. The protocol has exempted non-Muslims from the implementation of the *Sharia* law. But we have to be mindful of the fact that many Muslims criticize the implementation of the Islamic law in the North. For an interesting perspective on this issue see Abdulahi Ahmed An-Na'im (1990) *Toward an Islamic Reformation: Civil Liberties, Human Rights, and International Law*, Syracuse, New York: Syracuse University Press.
33. See John Garang (1992) *The Call for Democracy in Sudan*, edited and introduced by Mansour Khalid, London and New York: Kegan Paul International, pp. 26–27.

Chapter 6   Beyond "Race" and "Ethnicity": Toward a Transformative Discourse for Democratic Citizenship

1. For an interesting perspective on these issues see Mamdani "Indirect Rule, Civil Society, and Ethnicity."
2. Since its independence in 1956, the Sudan has experienced three parliamentary democracies (1956–1958, 1964–1969, and 1986–1989), and three periods of military rule (1958–1964, 1969–1985, and 1989–present).
3. For an interesting work on this issue see Harir, "Recycling the Past in the Sudan."
4. O' Brien, "Power and the Discourse of Ethnicity in Sudan," p. 67.
5. Francis M. Deng, *Dynamics of Integration*, p. 16.
6. See Marable, *Beyond Black and White*, p. 186.
7. See Muddathir Abd Al-Rahim (1969) *Imperialism and Nationalism in the Sudan*, p. 7.
8. Speech delivered by Mr. Aggrey Jaden on the Round Table Conference, 1965, p. 4.
9. See Wai, *The African–Arab Conflict in the Sudan*, p. 1.
10. See Ruay, *The Politics of Two Sudans*, p. 73.
11. Indeed, it would be a mistake to think that there is a unified political vision among Southern Sudanese, Fur, or the Beja.
12. Poluha, "Ethnicity and Democracy—A Viable Alliance?," p. 39.
13. See Masolo, "African Philosophy," p. 285.
14. The brutal political violence between the Nuer and the Dinka that occurred after the split of 1991 has shown how the legacy of indirect rule continues to haunt people of the Southern Sudan. Since then, fragmentation, individualism, and lack of a consensus characterized the political culture of the Southern Sudan. For a detailed study see Douglas H. Johnson (1998) "The Sudan People's Liberation Army and the Problem of Factionalism," in Christopher Clapham (ed.) *African Guerrillas*, Oxford: James Currey, pp. 53–72; also see Jok and Hutchinson, "Sudan's Prolonged Second Civil War," pp. 125–145.
15. See the statement by John Garang de Mabior at the opening session of the preliminary dialogue between SPLM/A and the National

Alliance for National Salvation, held at Koka Dam, March 20, 1986. Cited in *John Garang Speaks* (1987) edited and introduced by Mansour Khalid, p. 125.

16. See the statement by Sudan People's Liberation Movement and Sudan People's Liberation Army (SPLM/A), Department of Information, Ghaffar and Sorbo, "On the New Sudan," pp. 84–85.

17. See SLM/A Political Declaration, March 13, 2003, p. 3.

18. See Francis Deng's statement on the internal displacement crisis in the Darfur region after his trip to the region, published on Sudanese Online Discussion Board, August 3, 2004. Published in http://www. sudaneseonline.com.

Bibliography

Unpublished Primary Sources

Oral Sources
The oral sources used in this study were collected through interviews with Southern Sudanese refugees in Cairo, Egypt, during two fields trips totaling seven months in 1996 and 1997.

List of Informants
I have not used the real names of the informants in this list so as to protect the safety of the refugees.

1. Mr. Benn Duk
2. Mr. Nelson J. Deng
3. Mr. Joseph Adam
4. Mr. Hran B.
5. Mr. Samuel Ahmed
6. Dr. Nicola T.
7. Ms. Mary Edward
8. Mr. David Waya
9. Ms. Sara Frank
10. Mr. Sustin A.
11. Ms. Merriam John
12. Mr. Sebit Tutu
13. Ms. Susan Lunga
14. Ms. Rose Deng
15. Mr. Mohamed O
16. Mr. Francis J. Kuel
17. Mr. Samuel Wang

18. Mr. Akol Othem
20. Mr. Micheal William
21. Mr. Luk David
22. Ms. Asha Abate

Published Primary Sources

Books Containing Documentary Sources

The Upper Nile Province Handbook: A report on Peoples and Government in the Southern Sudan, 1931, compiled by C.A. Willis, edited by Douglas H. Johnson, Oxford: Oxford University Press, 1996.

British Documents on the End of Empire: Sudan, Part 1 and 2, edited by Douglas H. Johnson, London: HMSO, 1998.

Official Reports and Government Publications

A letter to Finacial Secretary, 29/3/22, SGA, Civsec 20/21/97.

Willis C.A., "Report on Slavery," 1926, NRO Civsec 60/2/7, p. 18.

A memorandum prepared on the request of Wingate, cited in Cromer to Salisbury, April 11, 1899, FO 407/151.

Lord Kitchener, "Memorandum to Mudirs," enclosed in Cromer to Salisbury, 17/3/99/ F. O 78/5022.

Letter to Civil Secretary on "Nuer Policy," dated February 18, 1929, NRO UNP 1/44/329.

General Statement of Policy in the Southern Sudan with regards to administration, religion, and education, 14/3/22, SGA, Civsec 1/9/3/.

Memorandum on Southern Policy, January 25, 1930, by Sir Harold MacMichael, Bahr al Ghazal 1/1/1.

Political Documents of Political Groups in the Sudan

Political Declaration of the Sudan Liberation Movement and Sudan Liberation Army (SLM/A), signed by Minni Arkou Minnawi, Secretary General, March 13, 2003, Darfur, Sudan.

Sudan People's Liberation Movement and Sudan People's Liberation Army (SPLM/A), Department of Information (1989) "On the New Sudan," in Management of the Crisis in Sudan, M.A. Abdel Ghaffar and Gunnar M. Sorbo (eds.), Bergen: Center for Development Studies, University of Bergen, pp. 84–85.

The National Democratic Alliance (NDA), *Documents of the Conference on Fundamental Issues*, Asmara, June 12–23, 1995.

Statement by John Garang de Mabior at the opening session of the preliminary dialogue between SPLM/A and the National Alliance for National Salvation, held at Koka Dam, Ethiopia, March 20, 1986. Cited in *John Garang Speaks*, edited and introduced by Mansour Khalid, 1987.

Speech delivered by Mr. Aggrey Jaden on the Round Table Conference, 1965.

South Sudan Resistance Movement, *The Anya-Nya Struggle: Background and Objectives*, South Sudan, SSRM, 1971.

Southern Front, *The Southern Front Memorandum to OAU on Afro-Arab conflict in the Sudan*, Accra, Ghana, 1965.

Unpublished Secondary Sources

Unpublished Dissertations and Papers
Carretson, P.P. (1974) "A History of Addis Ababa from Its Foundation in 1886 to 1919." Ph.D. dissertation, University of London, UK.

Edward, Jane Kani (1997) "Southern Sudanese Informal Groups: Obstacles and Strengths of Collective Activities among Southern Sudanese in Cairo." Paper presented to the Third International Sudan's Studies Conference, Cairo, Egypt, June.

Makris, G.P. (1995) "Construction of Categories from the Era of Colonialism to the Days of Militant Islam." Paper presented to a conference on nation-building in the Sudan, Cairo, Egypt, April.

Powell, Eve (1995) "Colonized Colonisers, Egyptian Nationalists and the Issue of the Sudan, 1875–1919." Unpublished Ph.D. thesis, Harvard University, May.

Published Secondary Sources

Periodicals
Sudan Democratic Gazette, November, 1996.
Hadarat al Sudan, June 25, 1924.
Southern Sudan Vision, April 1, 1992.
Southern Sudan Vision, No. 2, November 20, 1992.

Selected Books and Articles

Abd Al-Rahim M. (1969) *Imperialism and Nationalism in the Sudan.* Oxford: Clarendon Press.

Abdel Rahman, Mohamed (1973) "Interaction between Africans North and South the Sahara." *Journal of Black Studies*, 3 (2), pp. 131–147.

Abdel Salam, El Fatih A. (1989) "Ethnic Politics in the Sudan." In *Ethnicity, Conflict and National Integration in the Sudan*, Sayyid H. Hurreiz and El Fatih A. Abdel Salam (eds.), Khartoum: Khartoum University Press.

Adams, William Y. (1977) *Nubia: Corridor to Africa.* Princeton, NJ: Princeton University Press.

Adejumobi, Said (2001) "Citizenship, Rights, and the Problem of Conflicts and Civil Wars in Africa." *Human Rights Quarterly*, 3, pp. 148–170.

Africa Watch (1990) *Denying the Honor of Living: Sudan A Human Rights Disaster.* New York: Africa Watch, Human Rights Watch.

Ake, Claude (1973) "Explaining Political Instability in New State." *Journal of Modern African Studies*, 11 (3), pp. 247–259.

——— (1996) *Democracy and Development in Africa.* Washington, DC: Brookings Institution.

Albino, Oliver (1970) *The Sudan: A Southern View Point.* London: Oxford University Press.

Al Tunisi Mohamad Ibn (1851) "*Voyage.*" Cited in Mario J. Azevedo (1998) *Roots of Violence: A history of War in Chad.* Australia: Gordon & Breach.

Ali, Taisier M. and Robert O. Matthews (1999) "Civil War and Failed Peace Efforts in Sudan." In *Civil Wars in Africa: Roots and Resolutions*, Ali and Matthews (eds.), Montreal and Kingston: McGill-Queen's University Press.

Alier, Abel (1990) *Southern Sudan: Too Many Agreements Dishonoured.* London: Ithaca Press.

Allen, Chris (1999) "Warfare, Endemic Violence, and State Collapse in Africa." *Review of African Political Economy*, 81, pp. 367–384.

Alonso A. (1994) "The Politics of Space, Time and Substance: State Formation, Nationalism and Ethnicity. *Annual Review of Anthropology*, 23, pp. 379–405.

Alpers, Edward A. (1975) *Ivory and Slaves.* Berkeley: University of California Press.

Althusser, Louis (1971) *Lenin and Philosophy, and Other Essays.* Translated by Ben Brewster. New York: Monthly Review Press.

Anderson, Benedict (1983) *Imagined Communities: Reflections of the Origin and Spread of Nationalism.* London: Verso.

Anderson, G.N. (1999) *Sudan in Crisis: The Failure of Democracy.* Miami: University of Florida.

An-Naim, Abdullah A. (1993) "The National Question of Constitutionalism: Secession and Constitutionalism." In *Constitutionalism and Democracy: Transition in Contemporary World,* Douglas Greenberg et al. (eds.), Oxford: Oxford University Press.

Appiah, Kwame Anthony (1992) *In My Father's House.* New York: Oxford University Press.

Apter, David E. (1987) *Rethinking Development: Modernization, Dependency, and Postmodern Politics.* Newbury Park: Sage Publications.

Austen, Ralph (1981) "From the Atlantic to the Indian Ocean: European Abolition, the African Slave Trade, and the Asian Econmoic Structures." In *The Abolition of the Atlantic Slave Trade,* David Eltis and James Walvin (eds.), Madison: University of Wisconsin Press.

Badal, R.K. (1976) "The Rise and Fall of Separatism in South Sudan." *African Affairs,* 75 (301), pp. 463–474.

Badawi, Abduh (1973) *Al-Shu ara Al-Sua wa-Khasaisuhum fil-Shir al arabi.* Al-Qahiraha: Al-Hay ahal-Misriyah.

Baker, Bruce (1998) "The Class of 1990: How Have the Autocratic Leaders of Sub-Saharan Africa Fared under Democratization?" *Third World Quarterly,* 19 (1), pp. 115–127.

Bashir, Mohammed Omer (1968) *The Southern Sudan: Background to Conflict.* London: Hurst.

Bayart, Jean-Francois (1993) *The State in Africa: The Politics of the Belly.* London: Longman.

Bjorkelo, Anders (1988) *Prelude to the Mahdiyya.* Cambridge: Cambridge University Press.

Bratton, Michael (1997) *Democratic Experiments in Africa: Regime Transitions in Comparative Perspective.* Cambridge: Cambridge University Press.

Bratton, Michael and Nicholas Van de Walle (1994) "Neopatrimorial Regimes and Political Transition in Africa." *World Politics,* XLVI, pp. 453–489.

Brenner, Louis (1973) *The Shehus of Kukawa*. Oxford: Oxford University Press.

Callaghy, Thomas (1980) "Politics and Vision in Africa: The Interplay of Domination, Equality and Liberty." In Chabal (ed.) (1986).

——— (1984) *State-Society Struggle: Zaire in Comparative Perspective*. New York: Columbia University Press.

Chabal, Patrick (ed.) (1986) *Political Domination in Africa: Reflections on the Limits of Power*. Cambridge: Cambridge University Press.

Chambers, Iain (1994) *Migrancy Culture Identity*. London: Routledge.

Chole, Eshetu and Jibrin Ibrahim (eds.) (1995) *Democratization Processes in Africa: Problems and Prospects*. Dakar: CODESRIA Books.

Cohen, R. (1997) *Global Diasporas: An Introduction*. London: University of Central London Press.

Collins, Robert (1971) *Land Beyond the Rivers: The Southern Sudan*. New Haven: Yale University Press.

——— (1992) "The Nilotic Slave Trade: Past and Present." *Slavery and Abolition*, 13 (1), pp. 140–161.

Cooper, Frederick (1977) *Plantation Slavery on the East Coast of Africa*. New Haven: Yale University Press.

Cordell, Dennis (1985) *Dar al-Kuti and Last Years of Trans-Saharan Slave Trade*. Madison: University of Wisconsin Press.

Curtin, Philip (1978) *African History*. Harlow: Longman.

Daly M.W. (1980) *British Administration and the Northern Sudan: 1917–1924*. Leiden: Nederlands Historisch-Archaeologisch instituut.

Davidson, Basil (1992) *The Black Man's Burden: Africa and the Curse of the Nation-State*. London: James Currey.

Deng William and Joseph Oduho (1962) *The People of Southern Sudan*. Oxford: Institute of Race Relations.

——— (1963) *The Problem of the Southern Sudan*. London: London University Press.

Deng, Francis M. (1973) *Dynamics of Integration: A Basis for National Integration in the Sudan*. Khartoum: Khartoum University Press.

——— (1995) "Egypt's Dilemmas on the Sudan." *Middle East Policy*, 4 (1–2), pp. 50–56.

——— (1995) *War of Visions*. Washington, DC: Brookings Institutions.

Diamond, Larry (1988), "Introduction: Roots of Failure, Seeds of Hope." In *Democracy in Developing Countries: Africa*, Larry Diamond, Jaun Zinz, and Seymour Martin Lipset (eds.), Boulder, CO: Lynne Rienner.

El-Affendi, Abdel Wahab (1990) "Discovering the South: Sudanese Dilemmas for Islam in Africa." *African Affairs*, 89 (358), pp. 371–389.

Edward, Jane Kani (2001) "Southern Sudanese Refugee Women: Questioning the Past, Imagining the Future," in *Women's Rights and Human Rights: International Historical Perspectives*, Patricia Grimshaw, Katie Holmes and Marilyn Lake (eds.), London: Macmillan, pp. 272–289.

Eltis, David (1979) "The British Contribution to the Nineteenth Century Transatlantic Slave Trade." *Economic History Review*, 32, pp. 211–229.

Eltis, David and David Richardson (1997) "West Africa and the Transatlantic Slave Trade: New Evidence of Long Run Trends." *Slavery and Abolition*, 18 (1), pp. 16–35.

Ewald, Janet J. (1990) *Soldiers, Traders, and Slaves: State Formation and Economic Transformation in the Greater Nile Valley, 1700–1885*. Madison: University of Wisconsin Press.

Foucault, Michel (1980) *Power/Knowledge*. Colin Gordon (ed.), Brighton: Harvester Press.

Fredman, Steven (1999) "Agreeing to Differ: Africa Democracy, Its Obstacles and Prospects." *Social Research*, 66 (3), pp. 829–858.

Garang, John (1996) "The Shaping of a New Sudan." *Mediterranean Quarterly*, 74 (Fall), pp. 6–16.

Garretson, Peter P. (1986) "Vicious Cycles, Ivory, Slaves, and Arms on the New Maji Frontier." In *The Southern Marches of Imperial Ethiopia*, D. Donham and W. James (ed.), Cambridge: Cambridge University Press.

Gary, Richard (1961) *A History of Southern Sudan, 1839–1889*. Oxford: Oxford University Press.

Haggard, Stephen and Robert R. Kufman (1995) *The Political Economy of Democratic Transitions*. Princeton, NJ: Princeton University Press.

Harir, Sharif (1994) "Recycling the Past in the Sudan: An Overview of Political Decay." in *The Short-Cut to Decay: The Case of the Sudan*, S. Harir, and T. Tvedt (eds.), Uppsala: The Scandinavian Institute of African Studies.

Hassan, Yousif Fadl (1967) *The Arabs and the Sudan.* Edinburgh: Edinburgh University Press.

Hobsbawm, Eric and Terence Ranger (1983) *The Invention of Tradition.* Cambridge, NY: Cambridge University Press.

Howell, John (1973) "Politics in the Southern Sudan." *African Affairs,* 72 (April), pp. 163–164.

Hunwick, J.O. (1978) "Black Africans in the Islamic World: An Understudied Dimension of the Black Diaspora." *Tarikh,* 5 (4), pp. 5–37.

Hyden, Goran, Dele Olowu, and Hastings W.O. Okoth-Ogendo (eds.) (2000) *African Perspectives on Governance.* Trenton, NJ: Africa World Press.

Ibrahim, Hayder (1979) *The Shaiqiya: The Cultural and Social Change of a Northern Sudanese Riverain People.* Wiesbaden: Franzsteiner Verlag GMBH.

Idris, Amir H. (2001) *Sudan's Civil War—Slavery, Race and Formational Identities.* Lewiston: Edwin Mellen Press.

——— (2003) "Sudan." In *Encyclopedia of Twentieth-Century African History,* Paul Zeleza and Dickson Eyoh (eds.), London: Routledge.

——— (2004) "The Racialised and Islamicised Sudanese State and the Question of Southern Sudan." In *State Crises, Globalisation and National Movements in North-East Africa,* Asafa Jalata (ed.), New York: Routledge.

Jalata, Asafa (ed.) (2004) "The Process of State Formation in the Horn of Africa in Comparative Perspective." In *State Crises, Globalization and National Movements in North-East Africa.* London: Routledge.

James, Wendy (1990) "Kings, Commoners and the Ethnographic Imagination in Sudan and Ethiopia." In *Localizing Strategies: Regional Traditions of Ethnographic Writing,* Richard Fardon (ed.), Edinburgh: Scottish Academic Press.

Jok, Jok Madut (2001) *War and Slavery in Sudan.* Philadelphia, PA: University of Pennsylvania Press.

Jok, Jok Madut and S.E. Hutchinson (1999) "Sudan's Prolonged Second Civil War and the Militarization of Nuer and Dinka Ethnic Identities." *African Studies Review,* 42 (2), pp. 125–145.

Joseph, Richard (1997) "Democratization in Africa after 1989: Comparative and Theoretical Perspectives." *Comparative Politics,* 29, pp. 363–382.

Kamil, Abd-al-Aziz Abd-al-Gadir (1970) *Islam and the Race Question.* Paris, UNESCO.

Khalid, Mansour (1996) *The Government They Deserve: The Role of the Elite in Sudan's Political Evolution.* London: Kegan Paul.

Klein, Herbert (1978) *The Middle Passage: Comparative Studies in the Atlantic Slave Trade.* Princeton: Princeton University Press.

Kok, Peter (1996) "Sudan: Between Radical Restructuring and Deconstruction of State System." *Review of African Political Economy,* 70, pp. 555–561.

Lavin, Deborah (ed.) (1991) *The Condominium Remembered: Proceeding of the Durham Sudan* (vol. 1), Historical Records Conference. Durham: University of Durham Center for Middle Eastern and Islamic Studies.

Lesch, Ann Mosely (1998) *The Sudan: Contested National Identities.* Bloomington and Oxford: Indiana University Press.

Lovejoy, Paul (ed.) (1981) *The Ideology of Slavery in Africa.* Beverly Hills: Sage Publications.

Lugard, Frederick John (1965) *The Dual Mandate in British Tropical Africa.* (5th edn.), Hamden, CT: Archon Books.

MacMichael, H.A. (1934) *The Anglo-Egyptian Sudan.* London: Faber and Faber.

——— (1922) *A History of the Arabs in the Sudan.* (2 vols.). Cambridge: Cambridge University Press.

Mahgoub, Mohamed Ahmed (1974) *Democracy on Trial: Reflections on Arab and African Politics.* London: Deutsoh.

Mair, Lucy Philip (1936) *Native Policies in Africa.* London: Routledge.

Malwal, Bona (1981) *People and Power in the Sudan.* London: Ithaca Press.

Mamdani, Mahmood (1995) "Democratic Theory and Democratic Struggle." In *Democratization Processes in Africa,* Chole and Ibrahim (eds.), Dakar: CODESRIA Books, pp. 43–62.

——— (1996) "Indirect Rule, Civil Society, and Ethnicity: The African Dilemma." *Social Justice,* 23 (Spring 1–2), pp. 145–151.

——— (1996) *Citizen and Subject: Contemporary Africa and the Legacy of Late Colonialism.* Princeton, NJ: Princeton University Press.

——— (1999) "Indirect Rule, Civil Society, and Ethnicity: The African Dilemma." In *Out of One, Many Africas: Reconstructing the Study and Meaning of Africa,* William G. Martin and Michael O. West (eds.), Urbana and Chicago: University of Illinois Press.

Mamdani, Mahmood (2001) *When Victims Become Killers*. Princeton, NJ: Princeton University Press.

Marable, Manning (1995) *Beyond Black and White: Transforming African-American Politics*. New York: Verso.

Markakis, John (1987) *National and Class Conflict in the Horn of Africa*. Cambridge: Cambridge University Press.

Masolo, D.A. (1997) "African Philosophy and the Postcolonial: Some Misleading Abstractions about 'Identity.' " In *Postcolonial African Philosophy: A Critical Reader*, Emmanuel Chukwudi Eze (ed.), Cambridge, MA: Blackwell.

McClintock, David (1970) "The South Sudan Problem: Evolution of an Arab-African Confrontation." *Middle East Journal*, 24 (4), pp. 466–478.

McLoughlin, Peter (1962) "Economic Development and the Heritage of Slavery in the Sudan." *Africa*, XXXII, pp. 355–389.

Miers, Suzanne and Richard Roberts (eds.) (1988) *The End of Slavery in Africa*. Madison: University of Wisconsin Press.

Newbury, Catharine (1995) "Background to Genocide: Rwanda." *Issue: A Journal of Opinion*, xx (III/2), pp. 12–17.

Nyaba, Peter A. (1997) *The Politics of Liberation in South Sudan: An Insider View*. Kampala: Fountain Publishers.

O'Brien, Jay (1998) "Power and the Discourse of Ethnicity in Sudan." In *Ethnicity and the State in Eastern Africa* M.A., Mohammed Salih, Margaret A., and John Markakis (eds.), Uppsala: Nordiska Afrikainstitutet.

O'Fahey, R.S. and J.L. Spaulding (1974) *Kingdoms of the Sudan*. London: Methuen and CO.

Paris, Roland (1997) "Peacebuilding and the Limits of Liberal Internationalism." *International Security*, 22 (2), pp. 54–89.

Passmore, Lilian and Neville Sanderson (1981) *Education, Religion and Politics in Southern Sudan, 1899–1964*. London: Ithaca Press.

Poluha, Eva (1998) "Ethnicity and Democracy—A viable Alliance?" In *Ethnicity and State in Eastern Africa*, Mohamed Salih, Margaret A., and John Markakis (eds.), Uppasala: Nordiska Afrikainstitutet.

Reid, Richard (2001) "The Challenge of the Past: The Quest for Historical Legitimacy in Independent Eritrea." *History in Africa*, 28, pp. 239–272.

Reno, William (1999) *Warlord Politics and African States*. Boulder, CO: Lynne Rienner.

Ruay, Deng D. Akol (1994) *The Politics of Two Sudans*. Uppsala: Nordiska Afrikainstitutet.

Sachikonye, Lloyd (ed.) (1995) *Democracy, Civil Society and the State: Social Movements in South Africa*. Harare: Sapes Books.

Said, Edward W. (1993) "The Politics of Knowledge." In *Race, Identity and Representation in Education*, Comeron McCarthy and Warren Grichlow (eds.), New York: Routledge.

——— (1993) *Culture and Imperialism*. New York: Vintage Books.

Salih, Kamal Osman (1990) "The Sudan, 1985–1989: The Fading Democracy." *Journal of Modern African Studies*, 28 (2), pp. 199–224.

Salih, M.A. Mohammed, Margaret A., and John Markakis (eds.) (1998) *Ethnicity and the State in Eastern Africa*. Uppsala: Nordiska Afrikainstutet.

Sarap, Madan (1994) "Home and Identity." In *Travellers' Tales*. G. Robertson et al. (eds.), London: Routledge.

Sharkey, Heather J. (2003) *Living with Colonialism: Nationalism and Culture in the Anglo-Egyptian Sudan*. Berkeley: University of California Press.

Sikainga, Ahmad Alawad (1996) *Slaves into Workers*: Emancipation and Labor in Colonial Sudan, Modern Middle East Service, 1st edition (18), Austin: University of Texas Press.

Sorenson, John (1992) "History and Identity in the Horn of Africa." *Dialectical Anthropology*, 17 (3), pp. 227–252.

Spaulding, Jay (1973) "The Government of Sinnar." *Africa*, VI (1), pp. 19–35.

——— (1985) *The Heroic Age in Sinnar*. East Lansing: African Studies Center, Michigan State University.

Spencer J. Trimigham (1949) *Islam in the Sudan*. London: Oxford: Oxford University Press.

Sudan Cultural Digest Project (1996) "Coping with Dynamics of Culture and Change: The Case of Displaced Sudanese in Egypt." *Research Report*, no. 1, Cairo.

Wai, Dunstan (1973) *The Southern Sudan: A Problem of National Integration*. London: Frank Cass.

Wai, Dunstan (1981) *The African-Arab Conflict in the Sudan.* New York: Africana Pub. Co.

Warburg, Gabriel (1978) "Slavery and Labor in the Anglo-Egyptian Sudan." *Journal of Asian and African Studies,* 12, pp. 221–244.

Woodward, Peter (1981) "Nationalism and Opposition in Sudan." *African Affairs,* 80 (320), pp. 379–388.

——— (1992) *Sudan: 1898–1989: The Unstable State.* Boulder Co: Lynne Rienner Publishers.

Woodward, Peter and Forsyth Murray (eds.) (1994) *Conflict and Peace in the Horn of Africa: Federalism and Its Alternatives.* Aldershot: Dartmouth.

Young, John (1996) "Ethnicity and Power in Ethiopia." *Review of African Political Economy,* 23 (70), pp. 531–542.

Zartman, William (ed.) (1995) *Collapsed State: The Disintegration and Restoration of Legitimate Authority.* Boulder, CO: Lynne Rienner.

Zolberg, A. (1968) "The Structure of Political Conflict in the New States of Tropical Africa." *American Political Science Review,* 62 (1), pp. 70–87.

Index